THE CHILDLESS REVOLUTION

THE CHILDLESS REVOLUTION

Madelyn Cain

PERSEUS PUBLISHING

Cambridge, Massachusetts

For Paul and Elizabeth,
Heart and Soul

Copyright © 2001 by Madelyn Cain

Cataloging-in-Publication Data is available from the Library of Congress.
ISBN 0-7382-0460-9

Perseus Publishing is a member of the Perseus Books Group.
Find us on the World Wide Web at http://www.perseuspublishing.com
Perseus Publishing books are available at special discounts for bulk purchases in the U.S. by corporations, institutions, and other organizations. For more information, please contact the Special Markets Department at HarperCollins Publishers, 10 East 53rd Street, New York, NY 10022, or call 1-212-207-7528.

Text design by Tonya Hahn
Set in 11.5-point Janson by Perseus Publishing Services

First printing, 2001
1 2 3 4 5 6 7 8 9 10—03 02 01 00

Contents

Acknowledgments

Writers do not have the luxury (or punishment) of being locked away while they finish their work. They shop for groceries, get gas, and pick up the dry cleaning like everyone else. During crazed moments when they cannot do these everyday chores, others cover for them—and if they are lucky, forgive them for what does not get done. I was lucky. This book would never have been completed were it not for the full support of my husband, Paul, and our daughter, Elizabeth. They alone dealt with the moments when the computer crashed, I ran out of ink, or an interview had not been caught on tape. And those were the good days. They graciously allowed me to take time away from our family and put the energy onto these pages. My gratitude knows no bounds. Nor does my love.

My writing buddies, Lisa Gibson and Abigail Kelly, talented writers themselves, have made this book better not only by their editing skills but, more important, by their insights. Their suggestions proved invaluable.

Two professors from the University of Southern California gave me the courage to go forward. Dr. Gwyneth Erwin taught me how to edit and convinced me this book could be valuable. I have endeavored to make it so. Dr. Noel Riley Fitch, another extraordinary writer, offered the most practical advice at every step along the way. She prodded, pushed, soothed, edited, re-edited, found sources, and generally served as midwife. Without her generosity of time and talent, this book would not be what it is today.

Friends have offered constant support: Barbara, Kelly, Kathleen, Jana, Dan, Thea, Susan, Maggi, and our marvelous book club, thank you. Thanks also to my family: Mom, Mike, Julie, Catherine, and the cousins.

My agent, Denise Marcil, is to be thanked for believing in this project from the moment she saw it among the pile of others on her desk. She improved the book with her suggestions and I am grateful for her faith in it.

Marnie Cochran has been every writer's dream. Her enthusiasm and generosity as editor have served not only the book but my spirits as well.

And finally, to the women who opened their hearts and allowed me to interview them, thank you. I hope this book is all that you hoped, wanted, and needed it to be.

Madelyn Cain

Author's Note

About every six months, I have a dream that in essence is always the same: My husband announces to me, in some time frame before our wedding, that he does not wish to marry. The news devastates me. I am too old, I know in the dream, to find anyone else. Therefore, I will never be able to mother. In an instant, I am swirling, acutely aware of all that is lost to me. In the kind of reversal that only happens in a dream, the joys I have experienced mothering my daughter are sucked out of me in a blazing vortex and I keen for that which I cannot recapture and which is now denied me.

When I awaken, there is a moment of confusion when I fear the dream is reality. I quiet myself and listen to hear my husband breathing beside me. I pad down the hall to check on my sleeping child. Eventually, my racing heart slows.

I am not certain what meaning a psychologist might attach to this dream. For me, it is very straightforward. Childlessness was my biggest fear in life, and even now when I daily express gratitude for what I have been granted, I do not really trust it. It seems too good to be true.

Motherhood very nearly eluded me. I did not have my daughter until I was almost forty years old. Although many women now have babies at a much later age, I was nonetheless very close to the end of my so-called biological rope. The years between my twenties and when I finally had my child were permeated with an intense, unrelenting desire to mother. It was the strongest driving force of my life. I was anxious to marry and mother (in that old-fashioned order), but to my dismay the right man did not cross my path until I was thirty-one years old.

At age thirty-three, when we married, I began a round of surgeries and related procedures to ensure a pregnancy. Every month for the next six years, I suffered a staggering disappointment when I once again learned I was not pregnant.

I began to fear that perhaps a child was not in the cards for me and I panicked. Who would I be without a child, I wondered. How would I face the future without this deep need being met? I felt profoundly childless.

At the same time, I was surrounded by many friends who were ambivalent about having children. They drifted into childlessness without so much as a flutter. They had not planned on being childless, yet came to believe it was the right choice for them. Some friends were adamant about *not* having children. The very thought appalled them. They could not understand my desire and I could not (at the time) relate to their lack of it. They were perfectly content being childless.

A few friends fell in love with men who made it clear they did not want children. (Some of these men had children from previous marriages and were "done.") Faced with the choice of marrying a man they loved or gambling on meeting someone else in enough time to *possibly* have a child, they chose the marriage. Still other friends who had never considered children were suddenly responding to wildly ringing biological clocks. The race to fertility clinics was on! Sad to say, many of my friends were not as fortunate as I. Luck was not on their side, for reasons none of us can understand. They crossed into a world they did not want to be in. They were childless and devastated. And I ached for them.

I could not witness my friends' varied experiences and not be affected in some way. I began to bristle when hurtful comments were made about childless women. I knew these women personally. They were not the selfish, child-hating workaholics I saw references to in print, on television, and in movies. I resented the ways in which my friends were being defined. Even the women I knew who actively disliked children and were loath to be mothers were respectful of *my* choice. So why wasn't the reverse true? Why didn't the world treat *them* with the same respect?

The answer is complex. As a society, we have relied on a pronatalist (profamily) standard. We have been governed by it for more than 200 years. A review of tax laws makes clear that this is a government-sanctioned philosophy. If politicians are to be believed, this code is the very foundation of our great nation. But like it or not, our foundation is shifting.

For a variety of reasons—greater education for women, effective birth control, and later marriage among them—there has been a dramatic increase in the number of childless women over the past thirty years. Projected numbers are even more staggering. According to an article in *American Demographics*, there will be a 44 percent increase in the number of childless couples by the year 2010.[1] Childlessness is about to come bursting out of the closet.

As a society, however, we have not learned how to separate femininity from fertility when we define women. Childlessness confuses us and challenges our set beliefs. Therefore, it remains a prohibited topic. It has been easier (read: more comfortable) to ignore childlessness rather than face it. But the growing number of childless women is making that stance impossible to maintain.

When Betty Friedan wrote *The Feminine Mystique* in 1963, she identified a simple but profound need in women: the need to do meaningful work. The book became an instant best-seller because heretofore no one had been able to pinpoint "the problem that has no name."[2] Through Friedan's work, women gained not only an understanding about what was wrong, but also validation for the jumble of conflicting emotions they had been experiencing. Friedan's pronouncement broke ground; she brought what had been secretive out in the open. Friedan did not create a movement, but uncovered one. It was the first step taken toward redefining today's woman.

When I began writing *The Childless Revolution*, my goal was simply to put a face on childless women, not to make a major discovery about them. What I was not prepared for was uncovering a revolution in the making. Like Friedan, I discovered an unnamed problem: a reproductive choice that was not sanctioned by society, but was nonetheless being embraced with staggering momentum. Women, not society, were deciding what women wanted.

Childless women today are on the precipice of redefining womanhood in the most fundamental way ever. Entering the work force was merely the initial step toward redefining women—and possibly the first toward childlessness. The advent of the pill, the legalization of abortion, and advanced education for women were essential adjuncts to this change. The move toward remaining childless, however, is more profound, and will have more ramifications, than any step ever taken. For a society based on "family values," this shift toward an adult-centered world is historic. At its most fundamental level, the emergence of childlessness means that women are seizing the opportunity to be fully realized, self-determined individuals—regardless of what society at large thinks of them. They are fulfilling the promise of the women's movement, although that movement has neither acknowledged nor supported their cause.

What is most remarkable is that those spearheading this groundbreaking change are unmindful of their position. Like the women Friedan interviewed, the women I spoke with are not only unaware, but they feel they are alone; they do not know they are surrounded by a silent multitude.

Speaking the Unspoken

Recently, I have lectured on childlessness to women's studies classes at colleges and universities. The classes were filled with mostly younger women, but also included older students and a few men.

The response to the material I presented was electric. It struck a raw nerve. Students became extremely talkative—asking questions, sharing stories—in the discussions that followed the lectures. It was clear these students had never spoken openly about the topic before.

Each person in the room had a reason to be interested in the subject. Many of the young women were eager to articulate what had been rumbling around in their subconscious for a long time—that they were not sure they wanted children. But they had not told anyone. (These women mirror what women told Friedan, that they thought there was something wrong with them.)

Some of those who had children talked about the pressures put on them to conceive despite their own personal misgivings. No one had ever told these women that not having a child was okay. Or that they were part of a revolution. Everyone in the class knew at least one childless woman intimately, whether it was a friend, a sister, or a coworker. Generally, they knew many such women. It became evident in these discussions that there was a hunger for accurate information about childless women.

Redefining Childlessness

In researching this book, my quest was to uncover the truth about all childless women. The breadth of the topic was initially difficult to grasp, mainly because it encompassed such a variant mixture of women. I was also frustrated by the choice/chance distinction previously used to classify childless women; either a woman is joyous about her child-*free* state or she is devastated with her child*less*ness. I found this view too limiting to cover the entire topic.

Only through my speaking at length to childless women, and reading everything I could find on the topic, did the full picture finally emerge. Although some women actively chose childlessness and some tragically wound up that way, there are a great many in between: women who unexpectedly evolved into childlessness. These are women childless by happenstance.

In this group, positions alter with time or even with relationships. For example, a woman who may have wanted children finds the love of her life does not. She accepts this and remains childless. Another woman who imagined she would someday have children finds herself fulfilled by her work. She decides it would be unfair to bring a child into her life—she would not have the emotional resources to handle her career and a child—so she relinquishes her dreams of motherhood. This third classification, happenstance, had to be identified and acknowledged because it covers the group of women I believe will become the dominant voice of childless women in the very near future.

This book, therefore, is separated into the three classifications of childlessness: Choice, Chance, and Happenstance. Divisions within these sections identify the various reasons women remain childless.

In this book, I have adopted the terms "child*free*" for those who I thought were happy with their state and "child*less*" for those who were unhappy or even mildly ambivalent about it. I am dissatisfied with this simplistic terminology primarily because it defines women in the context of children, yet I failed—despite years of trying—to come up with words that were better suited. Perhaps a reader will have better luck than I.

The women in this book made either a decision about or an adjustment to childlessness. Each woman is without children for different reasons. Once you have heard their stories, you will wonder why there was ever any controversy, any judgment, or any proscription. They are, after all, simply women.

For those who are not childless, I wanted to dispel the fears, remove the ignorance, and correct the misconceptions about women without children. For families, friends, coworkers, educators, and therapists, I hope to provide useful insight into who childless women are and what their needs may be.

What Friedan did in her book was not create a movement, but uncover one. That is what happened here. The effect childlessness will have on society can only be imagined at this point. Certainly, as childless women become more vocal, accommodations will have to be made. Tax laws that discriminate against the childless through tax breaks to families, restrictive housing rules that force childless women to live in child-filled apartment buildings when they might prefer childfree living, patronizing doctors who refuse repeated requests to tie a woman's tubes, along with a host of other issues, will be challenged.

I am passionate on the topic of childlessness for various reasons. Being childless for many years, I dealt with others' assumptions (almost always inaccurate) about why I did not have children. I would like to see my childless friends have their dignity restored—regardless of why they are childless—by being able to talk about their state without having to justify it. I firmly believe this is the last great arena of feminism to remain unchampioned.

I wanted to write this book because in many ways a part of me still feels childless. I know, especially when I have my dream, that empty hole within. I knew I could tell this story, at least part of it, from the inside. I understood what being childless by chance was.

But that was only one part of the equation. The women who were childfree by choice embodied an inner peace I had rarely encountered before. In their experience, nothing was missing. Writing this book, I was reacquainted with the notion that my image of a happy life is not everyone's.

The women I met shared with me the most intimate details of their lives. I am humbled by their trust. Because I respect their privacy, I have used first names only. Only four women out of more than 100 whom I interviewed asked for a pseudonym. The words of these women are verbatim. I edited judiciously, but added nothing. I did not need to.

By walking into my fear and examining closely what life would have been for me without a child, I was hoping for a reprieve from my nightmare. I think I may have found it. These women taught me that life is rich in all forms.

M.C.

INTRODUCTION

"Society" may do as it pleases, since "the good" is whatever it chooses to do because it chooses to do it.

—AYN RAND[1]

Introduction

At my twenty-fifth college reunion, I sat at a table with seven of my best friends from school. Eagerly, we began to share all that had happened to us since leaving college.

Looking around, I remembered each woman as a young girl. I could conjure up her enthusiasm, her spark, her special gift. I appreciated the small lines on her face for what they were—the battle scars of life.

The petty jealousies we felt as college girls had long ago evaporated as deep affections rekindled. Marriages, divorces, memories, career upswings (or downsizing), marital infidelities, family deaths, and plain old aging united us.

How different we were from the girls who entered college in 1964. We had arrived at school in white gloves. We left covered in peace symbols and love beads.

The changes we underwent during those four years were more than the normal college transformations. The women's liberation movement, supported by the pill, altered the world into which we graduated. Although we

could not know it at the time, the changes were revolutionary. American family values were about to be permanently
altered.

As early baby boomers, we had grown up in a uniquely
comfortable era. Life was peaceful, prosperous, and pronatalist (profamily). Everyone by and large followed the same
proscribed formula: go to school, get a job, get married,
have kids.

This family values lifestyle was not new to the country.
In 1905, President Theodore Roosevelt, concerned that
immigrants were having larger numbers of children than
the citizenry, chastised the nation: "The primary duty of
the husband is to be the homemaker, the breadwinner for
his wife and family, and the primary duty of the woman is
to be the helpmeet, the housewife, and mother."[2] The men
and women who took to heart the admonition of the president became our great-grandparents. Our grandparents, in
turn, upheld the same set of standards.

The earliest serious breach to a child-filled nation came
during the Great Depression. Childbearing was at its lowest point ever. In 1929, the recorded birthrate was 21 percent. By 1933, it had dropped to 18 percent[3]—evidence
that the expansion of families was an option for only those
with the economic wherewithal.

In the 1940s, women left home to support the war effort.
With their men overseas, women kept the country opera-
tional. "At the start of World War II, 95 percent of women
workers intended to quit their jobs once the war was over.

By the end of the war, however, surveys revealed that more than 80 percent of women workers preferred to keep their jobs."[4] They did—or could—not. National spirit rallied around the soldiers, and wives and sweethearts left the workplace to make room for their returning heroes.

Influenced by media that supported the government's efforts to return to the status quo, the 1950s saw motherhood exalted. Commercials, television, and movies all coalesced to keep the nation on track. The most successful television shows of the day portrayed Donna Reed, Jane Wyman, Harriet Nelson, and June Lockhart as modern women happily devoted to their families. This glorification of motherhood continued into the early sixties, when a new crack in the societal wall became noticeable.

Experts disagree about the actual cause for the new women's liberation movement, which started in the 1960s. A variety of factors seemed to contribute. Some claim it began when the contented housewife stated she was not so content after all, as voiced by Betty Friedan in *The Feminine Mystique*. Friedan announced: "The picture of the happy housewife . . . is one of the semi-delusions of the feminine mystique. . . . For the women I interviewed who had suffered and solved the problem that has no name, to fulfill an ambition of their own, long buried or brand new, to work at top capacity, to have a sense of achievement, was like finding a missing piece of the puzzle of their lives."[5]

Friedan's uncanny ability to identify the source of women's malcontent emboldened many to come forward and state their own displeasure with the status quo. Daughters, observing their mothers' malaise, began questioning the touted joys of home life.

As divorce became socially acceptable, newly single women found themselves economically devastated and wondered how wise it had been to forgo a career in favor of staying at home. Young women, watching their mothers scramble to make ends meet, vowed they would live differently. They would not become economically dependent on any man. They would have careers.

Synergistically, effective birth control became available. The ability to have control over biological destiny was an enormous turning point for women. Without it, true liberation would have been impossible. With the fear of pregnancy now removed, women were free to choose a mate and the timing of their childbearing. The legalization of abortion was yet another essential component in strengthening women's freedom.

My generation came of age in the late 1960s. We were reared to be housewives and mothers, but ran smack into the sensibilities of the women's liberation movement. It appealed to our idealistic spirits. It made perfect sense.

So we forged a new path. Self-determination was our goal. No longer content to be defined as some man's daughter or someone's wife, we were eager to discover what it was *we* wanted in life.

And we did. I looked at my college friends and marveled at our diversity. Among us was a part-time office worker;

the head of a nursery school; a college president; a special education teacher; a stay-at-home mom; a lawyer; an executive with the government; and myself, a writer. Six of us had children, two did not. Three of us were stepmothers. Two were divorced, and one was about to be widowed. Two married in their early twenties (ironically the two who are now divorced), three married in their late twenties, and three of us married in our thirties. We were the personification of the liberation movement, the realization of all its promises.

I thought of my mother and her friends. Seven women also, but ones whose choices were few. All her friends married young; all had children. Only two worked. One was a nurse (the only woman in the group with a profession) who took assignments on rare occasion. The other was a divorcee with five kids whom she supported as a cocktail waitress.

My mother's crowd and my crowd are, I suspect, fairly accurate in reflecting our individual eras. The goal of women in the forties was to marry and have children. Women of the sixties wanted to be independent. In 1948, only 28 percent of college graduates were women.[6] By 1995, women made up 55 percent of the graduates.[7] The educations that passed our mothers by, we received. We were prepared for the careers they had forgone.

But as with all movements, there were downsides. Although the women of my generation were allowed the opportunity to create individualized futures, we mistakenly thought it in our power to control every aspect of our lives. And for that there was a comeuppance.

Emboldened by early successes, we assumed (never assume) we could have a child when we chose. But postponing motherhood proved unwise for some. Too often, delaying meant forfeiting.

I never once thought to ask the two childless women in my group why they were childless. Had they opted for this state or did they have no choice? They seemed content, their lives full. I knew them well enough to know they were fond of children (one was the college president), yet I did not know them well enough to know the whys.

Unlike the childless women of the past who either could not have children (and were pitied) or hated children (and were shunned), today's childless women are several different creatures.

Some women never wanted children. Although naysayers told them they would change their minds someday, they never did. They reached menopause content with their childless state.

Others, dropouts on the fertility merry-go-round, reluctantly came to grips with the reality of their situation, decided against adoption, and made peace with the fact that children were not in their future.

Some women, because of health or heredity concerns, chose not to have children. Some women married men who already had children and did not want to start another family. These wives transferred their parenting needs to their stepchildren.

Yet another group of women still hold on to their dream of one day having a child, although realistically they know the possibilities are slim. For them, grieving is ongoing.

With Oprah Winfrey as forerunner, the childless movement is gaining respectability. When Katharine Hepburn chose childlessness in the 1940s she claimed, "I was ambitious and knew I would not have children. I wanted total freedom."[8] Her views were thought to be scandalous. But when Oprah (a role model for many of today's women) admitted to *People* magazine "What it takes one on one [to parent], I don't have,"[9] she was not pilloried, but praised for understanding her own needs. Finally, it appears, childlessness is out of the closet.

In 1964, 13.2 percent of all women ages fifteen to forty-four had never borne a child. By 1976, the figure had risen to 35.1 percent—a jump of almost 200 percent in twelve years, despite tremendous advancements in infertility treatments. According to *American Demographics*, "The aging baby-boom generation will make childless couples one of the biggest growing segments of the next two decades."[10]

According to the U.S. Census Bureau, in 1993 there were 34.9 million American households that were childless compared with only 33.3 million homes with a child under the age of eighteen.[11] This represents the first reversal this country has ever made in childbearing. We are now trading families for nonfamilies.

Childless women today are on the precipice of redefining womanhood in the most fundamental way ever. Entering the workforce was merely the first step. What is remarkable is that those spearheading this change are unmindful of their positions.

I see the changes in my own family. My two grown step-daughters are in their thirties. I sit with them and their friends (eight women also in their thirties) as they discuss their options, or lack of them, with regard to childbearing. Their statistics are curious: All work, none is married, and none has a child. Although some of the women want a baby, they accept that they may either have to bear a child alone or forgo the experience altogether.

Most of these eight women are the products of divorced families. Their male counterparts, they complain, are reluctant to tie the knot. Often reared by mothers bitter from divorce and fathers with whom contact was limited, these young adults are founding the new unnatalistic society.

In her book *New Passages*, Gail Sheehy calls them the endangered generation: "Today many young people do not expect to be married until their late twenties, or thirties, or not at all. Singlehood is growing as never before."[12] Statistics support her claim. Between 1980 and 1996, there was more than a 19 percent increase in the number of women over eighteen years of age who had never married.[13] As a group, Sheehy claims, members of this generation do not choose a life course until they reach their twenties—ten years later than for previous generations.

This ten-year gap in development may be lamentable for the many women wanting children. If these women find a mate at all, it may be too late. Although this generation may not technically be endangered, future ones are seriously threatened.

These major alterations over the past three generations are revolutionary. The pattern set for hundreds of years now seems permanently altered. Childlessness is the tidal wave of the future.

According to the Census Bureau, in 1998, 42.2 percent of all women were childless. If this trend continues, and all indications are that it will, childless women will very soon be the norm, not the exception. We will no longer be a child-centered/family-oriented society. We will be adult-focused.

The leaders of this great transformation are today's childless women. Only by meeting them personally can we learn why they are childless and, in turn, where our country is headed.

I said good-bye to my college friends. We promised to do more than just send notes in Christmas cards. But we knew that would probably be impossible; our lives are too busy for the luxury of letter writing. We would e-mail on occasion.

Everything, it seems, is changing.

CHOICE

I do not breed well in captivity.

—GLORIA STEINEM[1]

1

Choice

Of the women who have actively chosen childlessness, I discovered three very distinct groups: those who are positively childfree, those who are religiously childfree, and those who are environmentally childfree. None of these women see themselves, or indeed their lives, as lacking anything. Their preference is to be referred to as child*free*, not child*less*.

Women who are positively childfree rarely express even a flicker of doubt about their decision. They range from those who love but eschew children to those who admit to actively disliking them. The religiously childfree are those who have made a decision to follow a spiritual path that requires they remain childless. These women voluntarily offer their childlessness as a manifestation of their devotion to their faith. Women who are environmentally childfree have made a conscious decision to forgo having children for the good of the planet. Their concerns, and their commitment, are passionate. Regardless of the cause, the results are similar; these women are decidedly childfree by choice.

Positively Childfree

On November 3, 1975, Ann Landers received a letter from a young couple undecided about having a baby. They asked the columnist to conduct a survey of her readers. They wanted to know, from parents with young children and older couples as well, whether parenting was worth it. "Were the rewards enough to make up for the grief?" they asked.

Landers took their request to her readers: "If you had it to do over again, would you have children?" she asked. The response? An astounding 70 percent of the respondents said no!

> I am 40, and my husband is 45. We have twin children under 8 years of age. I was an attractive, fulfilled career woman before I had these kids. Now I'm an overly exhausted, nervous wreck who misses her job and sees very little of her husband. He's got a "friend" I'm sure, and I don't blame him. Our children took all the romance out of our marriage. I'm too tired for sex, conversation or anything.
>
> Sign Me Too Late For Tears[2]

"I've lived for 70 years and I speak from experience as a mother of five," writes another. "Was it worth it? No. . . . Not one of our children has given us any pleasure. God knows we did our best, but we were failures as parents, and they are failures as people."

She signed her letter "Sad Story." Sad, indeed, and sobering.

One wonders how the young couple reacted to all this negative feedback. Did they heed the advice offered by the respondents? Or did they go forward, have children, end up regretting their decision, and then kick themselves for not listening to the advice they were given? Granted, an Ann Landers column can hardly be considered a valid scientific survey. And certainly the newspaper column itself has to be viewed in the context of the times in which it was published. The year 1975 found parent-child relationships undergoing a dramatic upheaval. Activist children of patriotic World War II parents were denouncing the Vietnam war, much to their parents' chagrin. Children, once reared in traditional religious households, were suddenly reveling in the sexual revolution, the advent of the pill, and the legalization of abortion. It is quite possible these were the disappointed parents who wrote in response to Landers's inquiry.

Then again, maybe not. Maybe parenthood is just not all it is cracked up to be, and some brave souls wanted (albeit anonymously) to spare others what no one had spared them—namely parenting.

In August 1998, a woman on the Internet offered this advice to a woman being pressured to have children:

Anybody that berates your decision to not have children are [*sic*] just jealous that you get to sleep, you are in charge of the remote,

you don't have fifty loads of laundry, your house isn't the neigh-
borhood 7-Eleven, and to top it off . . . you won't have home-
work!!!

I applaud your decision and wish I had the guts to make it 17
and 14 years ago, but NOOOO I had to listen to my mother and
experience the wonderful joys of motherhood. I should have just
rented the video.[3]

Clearly, unhappiness with parenting still exists.

In *The Hite Report on the Family*, Shere Hite reveals that
"mothers sometimes have children because they feel they
'should' have children; then they resent the restrictions and
duties that come into their lives, as well as the unequal burden of child care they bear . . . [and] many children feel
this anger is taken out on them."[4]

Ann Landers's respondents reinforce what the women in
the Hite report experience. Perhaps there is more unhappiness in parenting than has previously been admitted, which
makes one wonder why childlessness is not given more
credit as a viable option. Parenting is no longer a biological
consequence, but an option. All choices must be heavily
weighed, with each option given a fair share on the scale—
including childlessness.

You Are Not Alone

Until the time comes when childlessness is respected,
those who are childless must battle the prejudices and
preconceived notions of the pronatalist society they live

in. Leslie Lafayette's *Why Don't You Have Kids* defines pronatalism as "any attitude of society, any policy that is 'probirth' that exalts the role of parenthood, that encourages reproduction."[5] By implication, society condemns those who do not reproduce. Life can be lonely and frustrating for the childless. Finding others in the same boat helps.

One support group for childless couples and singles is Childless by Choice (CBC). Based in Leavenworth, Washington, its members afford comfort, information, and an occasional chuckle to fellow CBCers. Found in a recent CBC mailing was this quip: "Today's Lecture in Parenting 101: Why do you think God made boarding schools?"[6] Although humorous in nature, the core truth beneath the joke is clear: In America, a child shipped off to a boarding school is usually either troubled or unwanted. Wouldn't it be easier on everyone, particularly the child, if those who did not want children were encouraged (nay, even applauded) for not having them?

Childless by Choice is a haven for individuals who face a barrage of pronatalism on a daily basis. A leading organization that promotes the childfree lifestyle, CBC provides, among other things, reading material, legal rights information, workplace advice, essays on pertinent issues, and even suggestions on movies and television that reflect a childfree point of view.

Couples often feel pressured by those around them (parents, friends, coworkers, employers) to join the ranks and have a baby, whether they want to or not. Leslie Lafayette commiserates with these individuals. "A baby is a must-have accessory. . . . It is the finishing piece in every woman's life wardrobe. . . . Who can blame her for thinking she must have a baby?"[7] CBC exists because support is needed to fight this discrimination.

Lafayette renamed the childless "childfree." This term reflects an important distinction for those previously dubbed "childless" and makes clear that not everyone who is without a child is in mourning. For those for whom childlessness is a choice, this new phrase bespeaks their positive stance on the topic.

One woman related the following to me: "People say to me, you're married, you've got a house. . . . What's the problem?" It is as though childbearing were a given in every marriage. Hard though it may be to hear, some people simply do not want a baby. If 70 percent of those who responded to Ann Landers secretly loathed parenting, what makes anyone think that everyone should jump on the baby bandwagon?

A more recent Ann Landers column reflects the position of one couple who chose a childfree lifestyle many years ago:

You asked your readers to share their secrets for a long and happy marriage. My husband and I will soon celebrate our 40th anniversary, and we have had a wonderful life together.

Our formula is simple mathematics: one bed, two bathrooms and zero children. Selfish? Maybe. But it worked for us.

Landers replied, "Different strokes for different folks."[8] The 1950s (when this couple wed) saw the zenith of the baby boom; but unlike most married couples of the time, they resisted the trend and made the right choice for themselves.

"I Don't Like Kids!"

Luckily, some women never succumbed to outside coercion. Lauren, Wendy, and Sandy did not need an Ann Landers survey to tell them parenting was not on their to-do list. What the rest of society thought with regard to procreation never mattered to them. From an early age, each of these women knew she absolutely did not want kids. She never debated the issue, heard a biological clock ticking, or yielded to the inducement to mother. Unlike many of the women in this book whose childlessness is a complex issue, these women are childless for only one reason: They don't like kids. And they never did.

Disliking children is one of the strongest social taboos in existence. Not bearing a child is blasphemous enough, *not liking* them is tantamount to infanticide. Admitting it out loud takes either a foolish woman or a brave one. To reject the pull of the straight and narrow shows remarkable courage.

Lauren is one of those women. No traumatic childhood event led to her decision to remain childfree, but it is one she made early in life. "I grew up on *Leave It to Beaver* and *Ozzie and Harriet*, where for the woman [parenting] was your whole thing." Lauren sits with manicured hands carefully folded on the table in front of her. Jet-black hair swishes from side to side as she begins to tell her story. Her lipstick and matching sweater are vibrant red; dark eyes move in counterpoint to her hair.

"As a group, I don't like young kids." She fixes me with a level gaze. Her voice deepens. "I despise them. I don't like the screeching, the screaming, and the crying . . . 'give me this, give me that.' . . . It enrages me. Their voices irritate me." Her eyes drift toward the closed window. She shudders.

Although hers is an unpopular stance, Lauren is nonetheless comfortable admitting her position. When questioned about when these feelings may have started, she turns and looks at me. Her hands unfold on the tabletop. Fingers spread.

"When I was young, I had to take care of my brothers and sisters." She rolls her eyes. Reared Catholic in a home with five younger siblings, Lauren had her fill of children and caregiving. But many women, over time, change their minds, I offer. Didn't any romance ever tempt her to think otherwise, to reconsider? She shakes her head in an emphatic no.

"I ended two [serious] relationships over kids because there was no compromise." She refolds her hands and places them in her lap. At present, Lauren is forty-eight and has never married.

Lauren is on the extreme end of the childfree spectrum, but she is not alone. Each of us can recall women we have known who harbored an active dislike for children. Many of them were mothers. Although Lauren's childhood undoubtedly played a role in her decision, not everyone who took care of her siblings wound up hating children. We may wonder at her vitriol, but it is lucky for the children she did not bear that she remains childfree.

A Very Personal Decision

Most people would agree that whether or not to have children should not be an issue open for discussion with strangers. It is such a life-altering decision on the part of both parents and child that debate on the matter should be nonexistent. Either a child is or is not wanted.

So why would a couple seek advice from an Ann Landers column? Could it be that deep down this couple knew they did not want children but were afraid to follow their own instincts? Perhaps they needed support in their decision and turned to a newspaper column rather than family and friends who they feared might push them in a direction they did not want to go. Being childless was far more unpopular then than it is today. But far better to pass on parenting altogether rather than have a child you later regret, or even worse, resent.

Although not as fervent in her dislike of children, Wendy also admits she never wanted children. "I probably decided

I didn't want kids sometime when I was in junior high. It was no big deal. I just remember that every time the subject came up, I was put off [by it]. It's just not an experience I wanted. I still don't." She is a physically delicate woman, but her emotions are nonetheless strong.

"My family thought I was kidding. They didn't believe me at first. They told me I'd change my mind." There is a smile in her voice. "I didn't. I'm forty-six now, and I have no regrets."

The Eternal Maternal Myth

Is it possible there are women with no maternal instincts? So much is made of this trait, we have come to assume it is inborn. But is it? In *Mother Love: Myth and Reality*, Elizabeth Badinter asks, "Does the maternal instinct exist or is it an enormous put-on? . . . Instead of instinct, might it not be more accurate to credit the incredible social pressure that insists a woman can fulfill herself only through motherhood?"[9] To admit that some women are born without the supposed mothering gene seems incomprehensible. But it happens, perhaps more often than our society is comfortable admitting.

Bolstering the theory that perhaps some women are born without a mothering gene, researchers in Canada, England, and Japan have recently conducted research on mice that may have profound consequences. Their study was to determine if the maternal behavior of mice was affected by the lack of one particular gene, the Mest gene. Their conclusion is riveting. "Loss of Mest function is associated with two distinct phenotypes: intrauterine growth retardation and abnormal maternal response to newborns."[10] In other words, the babies born to non-Mest mothers were smaller than those born to mothers with the gene. They failed to grow at an expected rate. Also, the non-Mest mothers did not respond at birth to their pups in a normal way; they did not feed their young or nest them in the manner in which the Mest-gene mothers did. Although it is dangerous to extrapolate from this research to apply it to humans, these researchers came to this startling conclusion: "These findings have important implications for our current understanding . . . for the interpretation of previous genetic data, both in mice and humans."

Yet to date, no studies have been conducted on humans to determine if some women are Mest deficient. If the Mest gene could be identified positively or negatively in women, then all previous misconceptions about childless women would have to be abandoned. It would simply be a matter of nature, not choice. It would clarify why some women are indifferent to children and why some crave them.

Researchers say it is too dangerous or too difficult at this stage to conduct this kind of research on live candidates. Scientists have known about the Mest gene for some time, but the public has not heard about it. This is unfortunate, as this issue has profound consequences for childless women, most especially those who have been labeled child haters.

Only Aesthetically

Wendy might be a Mest-deficient woman. I ask her if the sight of a newborn tugs at her heartstrings, if a cooing, sweet-smelling baby arouses some primitive feelings.

Her tone is matter of fact. "Not really. Aesthetically, I like babies," Wendy admits, "but I think it's because they remind me more of animals. When they get to the age when they start asking questions, my circuits shut down *very* quickly."

Wendy is brutally honest in her self-assessment. Like Lauren, she is comfortable admitting to being child-phobic. She is also willing to broach another seemingly forbidden topic: "I cop to the fact that I'm self-centered and don't want kids."

Although selfishness is not a trait shared by the majority of childless women, for one group of women it is not only accurate, it is unabashedly acknowledged.

A frustrated Wendy admits, "I hate that adult choices are limited because of the needs of children. I hate that adult shows are put on television later, for example."

She sighs deeply, "Hey, if you wanted a recipe for someone who shouldn't have kids, it's me. One, I've always liked time alone, even as a kid. Two, I wanted an exciting career; and three, I wanted to travel to exotic places."

She smiles a Cheshire cat grin because she has achieved her goals; she contentedly spent time alone as a child, she is fulfilled and still fascinated by her career (first in the foreign service and now as an attorney), and she goes abroad almost every summer. Wendy knows what works for her: "Some people like red and some people like blue."

Sandy is also outspoken about her childless state. She says that from an early age, "I *never* wanted them. I didn't like kids." She leans in and whispers, "I'm a very impatient person and you have to be sweet and kind, and I'm very warm and caring but nobody's ever described me as sweet and kind." Sandy chuckles a deep, self-deprecating laugh. "And patient? I don't think so." She pulls back and laughs again.

When asked why she never wanted children, she shrugs, "It's just a missing gene. The clock never ticked."

I ask if people have ever accused her of being selfish. "Selfish? Yes." She chuckles, "Do I think that's bad? No. Look, selfish has a bad connotation to it." She thinks for a moment. "You know the word 'criticism' has come to have a bad connotation to it." She leans toward me and passionately explains, "It's not necessarily bad. You know, Roger Ebert can criticize [*sic*] a movie and only say *wonderful* things about it, but I don't think selfish has both sides to it. I think it's [only got] a bad connotation."

Each of these women is happy with the choice she made to be childfree. Sandy says as she leans back in her chair, "I feel very privileged to have lived the life I have lived and enjoyed the things I have enjoyed. I have been brave enough to live the life that seemed right to me."

One Choice Fits All

Preferring adult-only company is still considered practically un-American. But Wendy is right, I think: Some people like red and some people like blue. This should not be a one-choice-fits-all society. Children deserve to be wanted. If the people who do not like children were afforded the respect they deserve in making their own determination, the world would be less populated by children whose mothers dislike them. And fewer adults would have to undo the damage inflicted by uncaring parents.

One woman told me, "Why is it that we always feel the path to someone else's house will lead us home?" If a woman is to discover the path that is right for her, it may take going against the conventional grain to do so. To be "home," to be comfortable in ourselves and content with our decisions, takes valiant leaps of faith along the way—often into dark pools of unknown origins.

Choosing to live an authentic life means sometimes traveling down a path where there are few wayfarers, where the trail may be unmarked, and where there is no one to guide you on your way. But if, one day, you arrive at the cottage where the chairs and bed are, as Goldilocks says, "just my size," then the journey was worth it.

Religiously Childless

Some make life choices that demand that they never reproduce. A spiritual path may impose reproductive restrictions on its devotees that are embraced by the followers. Although the number of women who choose childlessness for religious reasons may be quite small, they nonetheless are one group of women who are often afforded respect for their choice.

Judy decided to become a nun while still in high school. On graduation, she entered the novitiate. She remained in the convent for over thirty years. "I really didn't think of it as being childless. I made a commitment to the service of God. There wasn't a childlessness about it. . . . The goal superseded any other desires I may have had, like getting married and having children. I was just totally dedicated to becoming a sister." Since leaving the convent, Judy has surrounded herself with children. She works in a grammar school as a computer teacher.

I wonder if Judy ever questioned her choice. "There were moments when I wondered if I had done the right thing. But I think anyone looks back and wonders, why didn't I do this or why didn't I do that? I think that's just human quarterbacking." Her only regret: "I wish I'd had kids that I could have shared with my sister." Judy begins to tear up. "So that we could have had families growing up together."

Agnes Stevens, also a former nun, is exceedingly dedicated to children. In 1993, she started the School on

Wheels, a volunteer tutoring project dedicated to homeless children.[11] Nuns and children, it would appear, are often synonymous—a curious confluence considering these women are consciously childless.

Although the Catholic Church demands that those in religious life (nuns, priests, and brothers) remain childless, other religious groups have either no proscription or only a suggested one. A few cults have been known to exert pressures on their members' personal lives that mirror the practices of some religious groups. Synanon, a group founded by Charles Dederich in the late 1950s, originally began as a drug and alcohol rehabilitation program. During the mid-1970s, the group underwent some significant changes, including Dederich's declaring Synanon a religion. Some expressed concern that the group, the members of which lived together in a communelike setting, had turned into a cult. One new idea Dederich began espousing was childlessness. He believed the group should care for the children of the world and not bring more into an already-overcrowded planet. Males in the organization were encouraged to have vasectomies. If you didn't, says Mark, a former member, "you weren't taken seriously—you weren't viewed as committed." Vasectomies were seen "as a rite of passage." In all, some 250 Synanon men underwent vasectomies.[12]

Many Synanon women spent a majority of their childbearing years in the group, which may have disbanded too late for those who wanted children. Unlike the nuns who understood the stipulation of childlessness imposed by

their religious choice, some of these women did not anticipate the childless directive that would develop after they
entered the group.

Environmentally Childfree

It may be hard to imagine a woman forgoing childbearing
for the greater good of the planet, yet thousands of women
have done just that. Their choice is fueled by a desire to
make the world a better place.

No childless women are as single-minded in their devotion to remaining childfree as those who have committed
themselves to the challenge of reducing overpopulation.
They are not only proud but often righteous in their
stance.

What sets these environmentally childless women apart
is that they are thought-based, not feeling-based, regarding
childlessness. For them, remaining childfree is a political
decision.

Oh, Baby

On October 12, 1999, with an air of jubilation, proud doctors held aloft a child touted as the world's 6 billionth
baby.[13] Newspapers ran photos and television broadcasters
cheerfully announced this historic event. But not everyone
greeted the news with unrestrained glee. Environmental-

ists the world over hung their collective heads, wondering when the madness would end.

Concerns for the environment, and overpopulation specifically, first gained public recognition in the 1960s. Founded in 1968 by Paul Ehrlich, Zero Population Growth (ZPG) was one of the first and most effective organizations in getting the message out. ZPG has been advocating reproductive choices since its inception. The organization counters pronatalist forces with frightening facts: At the current rate of growth, according to ZPG, the United States will more than double its 1940 population by the year 2050.[14] ZPG's concern is not simply a matter of where we are going to put all these people; it is a matter of the earth being able to sustain them. ZPG warns:

> Rapid population growth consumes forests and agricultural land, contributes to wildlife extinction, increases pollution and waste, exacerbates climate change, heightens competition for scarce resources, multiplies urban problems, contributes to economic and political instability, and threatens the health and welfare of present and future generations. Unless we can slow population growth, it will be impossible to address these and other critical social and environmental problems.[15]

The consequences of this anticipated growth is staggering. Viewed in this light, childlessness could well be seen as a noble calling. The childfree women in this section remain committed to the cause. They further ZPG's one-child-per-person replacement plea and go one better: They have no children.

The Individual Choice

Over coffee, I asked Deborah, a cheerful woman in her early fifties who recently returned to college, if she feels she has made a sacrifice by not having a child. "No. It's good for the planet! Overpopulation is our biggest problem and people are not acting in a responsible way. We are doing a service to the planet—those of us who chose not to have kids." She leaves her overstuffed chair in the coffee-house and places our plastic spoons in the recycle bins near the counter.

For many women, this awareness of the planet extends far beyond concerns for overpopulation. At twenty-eight, Eleni is firm in her commitment to the planet and to remaining childfree. She has known from an early age that she did not want children. Asked what environmental issue bothers her the most, she replies fervently, "Seeing the mountains being deforested! I just want to shout 'STOP BREEDING!'"

Susanna also mourns the ravaging of our forests. She tells me of a recent visit to a do-it-yourself store. The huge warehouse piled with lumber brought tears to her eyes. "I feel there's got to be a hole somewhere [in the forest] like I saw in the Arizona copper mines. The mines there are stripped and the hills are washed out. Childlessness is an offering to the universe. A repenting for humanity."

Although few individuals are as ecologically sensitive as Deborah, Susanna, and Eleni, their ranks are growing. It is difficult for these women to understand why the rest of the human race is so complacent about matters that threaten us all. Surely, we are aware the planet is being depleted, that more species become extinct each year, that pollution is destroying our protective ozone layer at an alarming rate, and that forests and lands are being heedlessly destroyed to make way for more people? The numbers on the U.N. population tote board keep soaring. These women wonder why more people aren't concerned.

The answer may be simple. Everyday life is so frantic for each of us—rushing to jobs, caring for loved ones, maintaining homes—that there is little time to learn about the myriad worthwhile causes we know exist. Reports now indicate that in the United States workers toil longer than any other individuals in the world.[16] Those women who have taken the time and explored the topic of overpopulation thoroughly, however, may find themselves compelled to choose childlessness.

Other Mothering

Linda is a fifty-three-year-old artist who chose to be environmentally childless when she was young. In a garden one afternoon, she discusses women's roles: "We have to rethink the notion that a woman has to have children to be considered productive and successful." She believes passionately that there is a purpose for everything in life—even childlessness. Linda perceives childlessness as "a blessing."

We talk for some time about her art and the beauty she creates—and how necessary it is for her to have unfettered time available to devote to her work—time she would not have if she had children. Nevertheless, Linda still believes that women, as nurturers, must offer their gift to the universe in some form. In a soft voice she tells me: "It is imperative to give the love a woman would have given a child and give it in other ways . . . to give back to life." She motions to the garden around her. "To treat the earth like it was your child."

Diane not only thinks childlessness is better for the planet, she believes her choice shows "a higher level of evolvement." Now forty-seven, Diane decided a few years ago to switch careers from dental hygienist to massage therapist. A tall woman with gentle brown eyes, she tells me she seeks to be the best human being she can be. Rather than loving just one individual, she believes in actively loving everyone she meets. Her choice of work is an outgrowth of her philosophy.

Jennifer is thirty, but knows she will never have children. She credits an "overarching socioeconomic belief about overpopulation" for her decision. She also believes Thoreau's tenet that man should leave the world a better place for being here, whether it be through improving a garden or educating someone or having a child. For Jennifer, *not* having a child is leaving the world a better place.

The notion of female-as-nurturer was expressed frequently by environmentally childfree women, but not in the traditional sense. To them, a nurturer does the unselfish thing. In their opinion, *having* children is a selfish act, one that does not serve the planet. *Not* having children is the generosity.

Eleni believes, "People are having children out of self-centered interests. *We're* thinking of the survival of the species. *We're* protecting society." Although this view may seem extreme, it is a sentiment I heard from many women. Separately, Susanna added, "I feel that 60 percent of the population is a mistake." Her feeling is that too many people have children without giving the decision proper consideration.

Making It Possible

The women interviewed for this book thought long and hard about having or not having children. Unlike women who accidentally get pregnant and become parents by default, these women recognize the importance of being a wholly committed mother.

This decision-making process would not even be a possibility were it not for birth control. Without the introduction of the pill in the 1960s, ZPG's goal would be an unat-

tainable dream. Thanks to the pill, and the changing atti-
tudes in women, our birthrates have been declining.

Although Americans may be having fewer babies, they
still consume more than their fair share of the world's resources. Susanna's concern is that "Americans are less than
10 percent of the global population, but we use over 20
percent of the raw materials. If everyone wanted to live like
us, it would be over in three years."

Robert Gillespie, a former board member of Zero Population Growth and now founder of Population Communication, had this to say:

> If you're congratulating yourself on being a Responsible Amer-
> ican with just one or two kids, don't. The paradox is that one
> American consumes as much as 60 Bengalis, as much as three
> Japanese, and twice as much as a German. . . . We are the most
> gluttonous country in the world, with no discipline economi-
> cally or politically. That's going to go on until there's a major
> crisis such as gas or oil running out. . . . We live in an artificial
> world, and nobody is addressing the future as it relates to finite
> resources. And all resources are finite—except population.[17]

Stephanie, a forty-seven-year-old college professor, sees
an irony in the reduction in children. "I think it's the ultimate capitalist joke: Industrial nations are having less [sic]
children in order to live a more materialistic life." She frets
that we are living heedlessly and the planet will pay the
price.

Although the escalation of the population strikes fear in the hearts of some, it echoes indifference in others. Hence why those committed to environmental issues are generally so forceful in their views—they feel *somebody* has to protect the world from itself.

ZPG's figures for the expansion of the U.S. population are accurate, but it must also be noted that the U.S. Census Bureau reports that nearly all developed countries (the United States, Europe, and most of eastern Asia) are steadily reducing birthrates to a point that may result in our not replacing ourselves. The study determined that it is the continued growth in developing countries that is causing birthrates to accelerate.[18] In 1998, the United Nations Population Division presented a report that verified that fertility rates around the world are increasing at a much slower rate than had previously been thought.[19] At present, the rate is 1.3 per female and sinking.[20] The United Nations Population Division (UNFPA) is now monitoring falling fertility rates from rich *and* poor countries alike. Somewhere along the line, the baby boom went bust.

The challenge—and push—is now on for groups like UNFPA to bring information about overpopulation to developing nations where the greatest growth is occurring.

Lessons from Abroad

Curiously, a good number of the women in this chapter who chose childlessness for the sake of the planet have traveled to many of these underdeveloped countries and have seen firsthand the cultural norms that often result in overpopulation.

Eleni worked for the Peace Corps in Honduras: "The people there were *very* family oriented." When they asked about her children and she told them she did not have any, "they felt sorry for me. They tried to reassure me [that I would one day have children]. It [the pity] is not that overt in the United States."

Diana's experience was somewhat similar. While working with the Peace Corps in Africa, she shocked women when she told them that she chose not to have children. "They would feel sad for me because I did not have children." To her, their reasons for having numerous children were clear: "They very strongly feel the need for large families because of the high infant mortality." But she sensed there was something more: "The difference in the African culture compared to ours is that there is a heavy cultural edict for children to care for aging parents. Even educated Africans are expected to care for [not only immediate family but also] their cousins."

Stephanie also visited Africa: "The women in West Africa saw me as a very sad case." Stephanie also was aware of the differences in family structure: "We don't have a culture that forces veneration of their parents. It is a cultural expectation in Africa."

Susan visited Africa as a student. She traveled with two professors and five other students. "We went to different villages and saw so much poverty, and lack of food, housing, and resources, and too many people. It made a real impression on me. I always thought I was poor growing up, but this was *way* different."

Witnessing firsthand the effects of overpopulation and a lack of resources had a great impact on these women and contributed to their commitment to remain childless.

Susanna did not have to travel outside of the Unites States to feel the same kind of pity aimed at Stephanie and Diana in Africa. While on assignment as a photographer in Nebraska, Susanna was introduced to local women who immediately wanted to know, "What does your husband think about your being here? Who's taking care of your kids?" When she told them she did not have any children, the mood became very strained. After three days with these traditionally minded women, Susanna decided to lie: "I told the women I couldn't have children and that was why my husband left me. The minute I became a victim, I was accepted." Although she hated the deception, it shows what length some childfree women have to go to neutralize a negative situation.

Susan grew up in Sitka, Alaska, part of the Klinket Indian tribe, a tribe that has inhabited the region longer than the Eskimos. They are a tight-knit community with strong belief in family. "People in the Native American community in my hometown keep asking me when I'm going to have kids. People don't believe me when I tell them [I'm not going to]. They worry, 'You're going to be an old maid.'" She senses their concern for her—but it has not dissuaded her from her stance.

Beyond the Pill

Although the birth control pill has been vital in giving women control over their reproductive choices, some women would prefer methods other than the pill and are frustrated in their attempts to obtain them.

Susanna did not want to use a contraceptive because "I didn't want to take the pill everyday because it said, 'I don't want children,' and I don't want to be reminded every day." From age twenty-four to thirty-five, she attempted to have a tubal ligation, but was thwarted repeatedly in her efforts to have the procedure done. She traveled to Sweden, Holland, and Switzerland and was turned down in each country, usually because doctors felt she was too young to make the decision. "The fourth time I tried was in the U.S. and they agreed to do it [only] because I was thirty-five, married, and my husband had two children. What annoyed me was that I had had a boyfriend who at age thirty-two walked in and got a vasectomy—*no problem!*"

Rosemary Gillespie, who wrote her doctoral thesis on childlessness in England, found that women in her country also had difficulty finding a doctor who would sterilize them. One woman she interviewed said: "I resented it [their presumptions] because it suggested that I didn't know my own mind. My own judgement was flawed. . . . I was not an adult." Said another woman, "I want to be sterilized but they just won't have it, because I'm too young . . . I am too young to know what I want, if what I want is not to be a mother. It would be different if I wanted to be a mother. I would not be too young then."[21] Childless women, Gillespie observed, were treated like children.

Sterilization might still be difficult for women to obtain, but there is new help in the area of birth control, a new generation of treatment called Preven, which prevents a pregnancy, rather than ending one. It is the first emergency contraceptive product that can be used postcoitally, or the "morning after." This remarkable drug received approval from the Food and Drug Administration (FDA) in 1998 but has received almost no publicity. Emergency contraceptive pills (ECPs) consist of four pills and work in one of three ways: They delay or prevent ovulation, they prevent the fertilization of the egg if it has been released from the ovary, or they create changes in the uterine linings to prevent implantation. Unlike the controversial RU-486, which has been targeted by many antiabortion groups, ECP does not abort a fetus. "The regimen consists of two doses of oral contraceptive. . . . The first dose of two pills is taken 72 hours after unprotected intercourse with the second dose following 12 hours later."[22] One of the drawbacks of Preven was the side effects: nausea and vomiting in some women. The latest incarnation of ECPs, which works the same way but has fewer side effects, is called Plan B (as in, "If Plan A—abstinence—didn't work, go to Plan B").[23] At present, the state of Washington allows pharmacies to dispense the pills to patients who have not seen a doctor. Other states are considering adopting similar measures. Groups like Planned Parenthood hope that Plan B will eventually be available over-the-counter to any woman who wants it.

Because this new method of birth control can be used after intercourse, it expands a woman's options even further. She can now be spared the fear of an unplanned pregnancy and the sometimes gut-wrenching experience of abortion. Each year, there are more than 3 million unintended pregnancies in the United States alone, and 1.4 million of them end in abortion.[24] Plan B will mean more control for women over reproduction, fewer unwanted pregnancies, and an undoubtable increase in the number of women who remain childless by choice. The Pacific Institute for Women's Health has been advocating education about, and distribution of, this postcoital secret. Francine Coeytaux, cofounder of the Institute, wants women to have this method as an option but warns that effectiveness does vary with the type of pill used. ECPs reduce the risk of pregnancy by 75 percent. Although not completely failproof, they are nonetheless another safeguard for women wishing to remain childfree. Coupled with RU-486, which has now received FDA approval in the United States, women now have private and safe alternatives.

CHANCE

We women made a mistake, I thought now, of not emphasizing the gift of being female.

—ANNE TAYLOR FLEMING[1]

2

Chance

It can be painful for a woman with medical difficulties to recognize that she does not have the physical capacity for the job of mothering. With the onset of illness or the realization of physical limitations, a woman's dreams may have to be abandoned, her goals retooled. Life can be challenging for those who must accept physical limitations imposed by nature or poor health, especially in a world that venerates self-determination. Family and friends may lend support, but the ultimate adjustment is made in private.

This section examines three groups of women who are childless by chance. First, it looks at women for whom disease makes mothering impossible, potentially dangerous, or physically challenging. A debilitating disease affects every decision in your life, including whether or not you can, or should, have children. Although many of these women are capable of childbearing, they do not feel physically or mentally up to the task. They are medically childless.

Gay women experience a unique problem when contemplating motherhood. They may physically be capable of achieving a pregnancy, but the issue of how to get pregnant, or even adopt, is complex.

The number of women with fertility problems is on the rise. They are differentiated from the medically childless because they share one common cause for childlessness: infertility. Although significant medical breakthroughs have been made in this field, the true rates of success at fertility clinics are not what prospective patients expect, or want, to hear. Sensationalized news of multiple births (due to the use of fertility drugs) gives false hope to the thousands of women who flock to these doctors with the hope of solving their conception problems. When treatment is unsuccessful, women anxious to mother find themselves tragically childless.

These three categories of women remain childless due to issues beyond their control.

Medically Childless

Carol is a talented artist whose home is filled with her own Chagall-like paintings. She opens the door in leopard pajamas, seated in her motorized wheelchair. She is having a bad day, so the interview takes place with her in bed.

For the past nine years, Carol has been battling multiple sclerosis (MS). In an ironic twist of fate, Carol was diagnosed at the same time she was awarded her marriage, family, and child counseling degree. During the first eight years of her illness, Carol worked with children as a therapist. She especially enjoyed getting down on the floor with her young patients and playing with them. It helped the children open up to her.

Most people with MS are diagnosed between the ages of twenty and forty—prime childbearing years. Doctors are not sure what causes MS, a chronic disease that affects the central nervous system. And although a woman with the disease may be physically capable of bearing a child (and many do), the concern for most patients is whether they will be up to the task of both bearing and caring for children.

Carol stopped working when she saw her patients were more concerned about her condition than their own. Her condition has advanced in the year since she stopped working; it has affected even her beloved painting. No longer able to hold a brush steadily, Carol now paints with her fingers.

Despite her apparent fondness for children, the time never seemed right for Carol to have them. Today, she has mixed feelings about not having them: "I would like to have them, but I don't think [now] I could handle it physically. I don't think I could give it my best." She smiles wryly. "I'm only good on a short-term basis."

Norrie is a research geologist and microbiologist with a doctorate in geosciences. Her view of childlessness is informed by her profession as well as her personal experience. Presently, she works in the coalfields of West Virginia, Pennsylvania, and Ohio, assessing the effect of bacteria on minerals. She observes that in nature, "we are genetically preprogrammed to reproduce . . . but the only place one actually has to insert a thought process is in making a decision *not* to reproduce—the cultural and the genetic messages are so very strong that you need real mental toughness to fight against these."

Norrie loves her life, her work, and her husband. She married at thirty, and three years later, due to an inherited medical condition, her doctor recommended a hysterectomy. The decision about whether or not to have children was made for her.

Diminished Capacity

Katherine is a tall, flaxen-haired woman from Montana with an easy laugh. "I never got the message that I *had* to get married and have a kid. I never even had a burning desire to have a kid. Maybe idealistically I did, because that's just a part of your life and you want to experience it, but the reality of my life and not having a boyfriend . . . it's the dichotomy of idealism and reality." She shrugs.

She told me that negative judgments about her childless state still exist: "If it [childlessness] is not an act of God, then [you're] selfish for thinking of your needs over creating a new life. There's a double standard. They come down on women who don't have kids, but men just get to have a life."

Katherine had a partial hysterectomy several years prior to our interview, which caused her to go into mourning. She explained: "The grieving came because I didn't have the choice anymore. Losing control, something I knew I could choose if I wanted to, was gone." But most painful of all to her was her boyfriend's reaction. "I saw the look in his eyes when I told him I couldn't have children. All of a sudden, it was time to move on. I saw it in his eyes. I was more upset about his attitude and betrayal because I felt diminished as a human being. I felt like damaged goods and worthless."

Anita always wanted children. When she moved to Portland, Oregon, she joined a singles group with the hopes of finding someone with the same desire. Much to her dismay, she discovered that everyone in the group was much younger than she. "I wondered, where do I fit in?" Before long, however, Anita's concerns were more crucial than merely where she would fit in. "I had just turned forty in February and was facing the likelihood that my biological clock was ticking down. I mourned the idea of not having a family." She takes a deep breath. "But I think God was preparing me for what was coming." In 1997, Anita was diagnosed with ovarian cancer. Her dreams of ever having a baby were suddenly over. "The doctor and I talked about the treatments and the surgeries. I cried a lot. The next day I was past that. I wanted to know, *how do I live?* I was mourning my birthday in February, and by May, I wanted more of them."

Anita's spiritual faith helped her accept what happened. "God's word tells us 'He works all things together for our good.' I can rest in the fact that He'll bring good out of this." Now forty-two, Anita comforts herself with the notion that if she did meet someone, she could always adopt. But she is also aware of a change within herself: "I have a lot less energy now, especially after the chemo. There's a certain amount of tiredness that never goes away." Nonetheless, she believes she is where God wants her to be.

Cris was born with a form of cerebral palsy: "In 1952, I don't think they even knew what to call it." Although physically capable of childbearing, Cris has motor coordination problems that affect her left arm and leg. When she married her husband at age thirty-two, they decided not to have children. Now that she is older, she says she has no second thoughts other than, "I regret not being able to raise someone with strong moral values. I would like to see a combination of my husband and myself."

Cris is extremely close to her nieces and nephews. "It's quasi-parenting. I enjoy the good without the pain." But Cris admits to some concerns about who will care for her when she is elderly.

In Sickness and in Health

For KJ and her husband, Douglas, the vow "in sickness and in health" was sorely tested, right from the beginning of their marriage. KJ was twenty-six when they wed. She and her husband anticipated that after about ten years of marriage they would have children. Two and a half weeks after her wedding, KJ was involved in a serious work-related accident. Her head injury was compounded when she developed posttraumatic fibromyalgia; neurochemicals at the base of her brain now send pain messages throughout her body, even to areas where there is no specific injury. KJ spent the first five years of her marriage in bed, dealing with immobilizing headaches and pain that continue to this day. For the first six months after the accident, KJ told her husband she would give him a divorce. One day he said, "Never tell me that again." She has not. It has been seven years since the accident.

Having children is out of the question for KJ and Douglas. "Feeling the way I do is rough on the people around me. I see the effect it has on my nieces and nephews. It would be too hard on kids." These days, the struggle to simply get around demands all of KJ's efforts. Her energies are now focused on finding a career that can accommodate her illness—a job that will allow her to work from home during her good hours and rest when she is unable to continue. KJ has returned to school and is beginning to piece together a new life, one she had not anticipated—a life that will not include children.

Gay and Childless

It is often assumed that most lesbians do not want children. Yet the gay women I spoke with expressed the same variant desires for children that heterosexual women share; some wanted them whereas others did not. Elizabeth explained her thoughts on why some gays may remain childless: "Sometimes a factor in what you want is a matter of what you can have. [A lesbian] may not let herself acknowledge how much she wants children just because she knows she can't have them." Jamie clearly wanted them: "I was raised in an extremely traditional culture, expected to marry and raise a large brood of Mormon children. When I finally recognized that God was not going to rescue me from my love for women and that this excluded me from the heart of the world I'd always thought I'd inhabit, becoming a mother seemed just another heart-rending loss I'd have to accept." Jamie has always cared for children. "My eyes are involuntarily drawn to that youngest human in the place, drinking in the soft eyes and miniature features."

In many ways, gay women share the same plight as couples who are infertile. They have a problem getting pregnant. For most lesbian women, the question is just how is that egg going to meet that sperm?

In vitro fertilization is an option, and a lesbian woman may chose to acquire donor sperm from a sperm bank. But the cost for these procedures can be high, and it rises exponentially each time the procedure is unsuccessful. Elizabeth spent two years and close to $25,000 on infertility treatments. She says she became almost suicidal on the fertility drug Clomid. When several treatments failed using donated sperm and her egg, the doctors suggested she go to the next level of treatment and use a donated egg. The thought of using a donor egg and sperm made Elizabeth think more seriously about adoption. After all, she would have no more biological connection to a donated sperm/egg child than she would an adopted child. Plus, going back on the fertility drugs held little appeal for her. Friends had also expressed concern about how she would handle an even longer period of time on drugs. Elizabeth had a greater concern: "I would have to use every last penny I had, and if that didn't work, I wouldn't have any money left to adopt." In the end, Elizabeth chose adoption.

Luckily for her, she was not in a relationship at the time. In a twist of irony, adoption can be difficult for a gay woman in a committed relationship. Rather than establishing a healthy home environment, a committed relationship opens the door to questions. Social workers conduct home studies to ascertain the suitability of the adoptive parent(s). The home of a gay couple is not considered by some as the ideal placement for a child. Elizabeth explained, "There are some gay-friendly agencies out there who adopt a 'don't ask, don't tell' approach." Thus Elizabeth's homosexuality was never indicated on her adoption papers. She was simply categorized as a single woman. If, however, Elizabeth had a mate when the visit was made, the agency would have been obligated to explore the relationship. "And that may have closed me out." Since Elizabeth had chosen to adopt internationally, it was important that her sexual preference be kept secret. She was told that in China, for instance, adoptive parents are now required to sign an affidavit that they are not homosexual. Elizabeth wanted an international adoption because she did not want the scrutiny she would encounter in the United States. "In a domestic adoption, the mother chooses the family. If you're a single woman competing for a healthy, Caucasian child, your chances are very slim." Ari, a gay woman wishing to adopt, spoke about the unique difficulties for gays with domestic adoptions: "In Florida, it's illegal [for a lesbian to adopt]. In Utah, it's nearly impossible." In foreign adoptions, a child is not available for adoption until both parents' rights have been terminated, or, in other words, when no one is going to change his or her mind and keep the baby, which sometimes happens in domestic cases. Once a woman has been approved for an international adoption, she will eventually be placed with a child. For a woman like Elizabeth, who had just been through fertility treatments, that sense of certainty that she would indeed wind up with a child was important.

To circumvent these adoption issues, some gays have intercourse with a male friend (often a gay man interested in fathering) or use a friend's donated sperm for in vitro fertilization. This, however, means the introduction of another biological parent, which can raise legal concerns, particularly for a gay couple wanting to raise a child on their own. But finding donors is not always easy. Jena tried artificial insemination with sperm donated by a male friend. After a few tries, when Jena was unsuccessful in getting pregnant, the man refused to donate more sperm.

Shari and Valerie are hoping to one day have a child. In California, where they live, a procedure called second-parent adoption is available. This allows both women to be named as coparents. But the decision for a gay couple to have a child presents yet another consideration, they told me, that of outing themselves and their families on a whole new level. Valerie told me, "A family which lives far away can tell people you have a roommate, but having a child presents a new set of problems for them." Although the couple may be willing to take this step, the same may not be true for their families. "The ramifications are that not everyone in your family may be as excited about your having a baby as they would be with a heterosexual couple," Shari explains. Some women may abandon thoughts of motherhood, knowing their families cannot handle their choice.

Complicating matters further are the legal difficulties of same-sex parenting. Susan has coparented her partner's biological child for ten years. But under her state's law, she is not allowed to formally adopt the child unless the mother relinquishes her own parental rights. The child is not entitled to Susan's social security benefits, nor is she covered by her insurance.

Given these major hurdles, it is little wonder that many gay women who wish to mother do not.

Jamie told me, "Now that I've passed forty . . . I feel my diminished physical energy unequal to the arduous task of full-time parenting." Yet she goes on to admit, "I still watch children wherever I go."

Tragically Childless

In a rural town in Minnesota, a lovely home sits on a quiet street surrounded by a well-tended lawn. In the garden, amid bluebells and lilies of the valley, a grave awaits the funeral due to take place. After the burial, baby's breath will be planted on top of the minuscule plot as a symbolic reminder. There is a delay, however, while a woman prepares herself for the finality of it all. Although she knows the time has come, she is having a hard time reconciling herself to the ceremony.

Unlike other funerals, there is no rush with this one, for there is no actual body, only the ghost of a child who never was and whose nonexistence has caused the mother-in-waiting untold grief.

The burial is Donna's idea. She hopes it might help finalize this long period of mourning and help her move on with life. Instead of a casket, there is simply a letter written to the son or daughter she never bore, telling of her deep love for the child; of her many plans for it; of the grandparents who looked forward to meeting it; and of the Christmases, Easters, graduations, and Sunday suppers—a life in general—of which the child and mother will never be a part. The gravestone is a small rock with the word DREAMS carved into it. For that is what Donna needs to bury: her dreams of ever having a child of her own.

Donna is not alone in her grief. In the United States, one out of every ten couples struggles with infertility.[2] Despite the many publicized successes in infertility treatment, assisted reproductive therapy still posts far more failures than successes. Even in vitro fertilization, which accounts for 70 percent of all fertility work done in the United States, can claim only one in five treatments as successful.[3] Four out of five women who undergo in vitro go home without a baby. These are women who craved motherhood, expected motherhood, and tried everything in their power to achieve motherhood—but ultimately were denied it.

The National Survey of Family Growth reported that in 1988 the percentage of women ages fifteen to forty-four who could not achieve a pregnancy was 8 percent. By 1995, that figure rose to 10 percent. In absolute numbers, the increase went from 4.6 million women to 6.2 million, an astonishing rise in so short a period of time. The number of couples with fertility problems grew by nearly 30 percent, from 2.1 million to 2.7 million.[4]

But not all women experiencing difficulty go for treatment. In 1995, the number of women who actively sought help for their infertility stood at 1.2 million—only half the total number affected.[5] Generally speaking, the women who did seek help were older, had a higher income, and were more likely to be married than those who did not seek medical help.

Indeed, contrary to common belief, infertility is not restricted to older women. In 1993, the percentage of women experiencing fertility problems broke down as follows: For women fifteen to thirty-four years old, the rate was 17.2 percent; for those thirty-five to forty-four years old, it was 21.4 percent.[6] This small 4.2 percent differential demonstrates that infertility bridges the generational gap.

The reasons for the rise in sterility are multifaceted. Women's careers, late marriages, and delayed childbearing all have an impact on the trend. These days, even environmental factors are being identified as possible causes for a woman's inability to bear children, even in younger women. In a report compiled by the Research Institute at the University of South Florida titled *The Environmental Causes of Infertility*, Dr. Wayne Sinclair cites cigarettes, alcohol, coffee, pesticides, food additives, aspartame, cosmetic chemicals, geographic locations, vehicle exhaust, and job occupation exposure as some of the reasons for infertility.[7] His theories are supported by a May 1997 article in the prestigious medical journal *Lancet*. Whether Sinclair and *Lancet* exaggerate or justifiably pinpoint one of the causes will probably continue to be debated. What is not disputed is that infertility is on the rise.

Although infertility is becoming a more prevalent occurrence, public perception about the problem is at best vague and at worst inaccurate. Most women still see infertility as a solvable problem. But for the most part, it is not. It is often not until a woman sits face to face with her gynecologist when she suspects a problem that she first hears the grim realities.

For women who have chosen to wait for motherhood, infertility problems come as a shock. According to Dr. Richard Marrs, one of the world's leading fertility experts and a pioneer in the field, "Most of the women I see have postponed getting pregnant almost universally because of their careers. They never thought they couldn't get pregnant. They're flabbergasted because they could achieve everything else they set out for and they're stunned they can't do this." Unlike his colleagues who cater to a younger clientele, half of the patients Marrs attends to are over forty years of age. He concedes there is a challenge in treating older women:

From the onset you have to realize that the fecundity rate [ability to produce] drops rapidly when a woman ages. For example, when a woman is 34 years old her fecundity rate is 20 percent per cycle. By age 44 it's 5 percent per cycle. But even if that 44-year-old does conceive, the miscarriage rate goes up. Her miscarriage rate is about 35 percent. Under 35 years of age the miscarriage rate is only 15 percent. And it's not so much a woman's system as the age of the eggs that creates the anomalies.[8]

In *New Passages*, Gail Sheehy writes that these older women suffer from what she calls the "fantasy of fertility forever":

The new Scarlett O'Hara is the high-achieving woman of 40 who tells herself, "Oh, fiddledeedee, I'll just think about getting pregnant tomorrow." If the marriage doesn't work out, or her career is too exciting and fast-paced even to think about making time for a toddler, she can turn off the biological alarm clock and rely on technology to bail her out when and if the desire surfaces.[9]

Although the older patient is surprised by her difficulties, the average, healthy twenty-five-year-old is flabbergasted to discover she needs the services of someone like Marrs. Like her more mature counterpart, she meets with experts anticipating unequivocal success. Yet fertility doctors, to the surprise of many women, can only do so much. Granted, in many cases these doctors have wrought genuine miracles; 20 percent of women who would *not* have borne a child without their help are now mothers. But in a business that is still highly unregulated, caution seems to be the watchword for those seeking help.

Cognizant of consumer concerns and aware of the negative publicity unscrupulous doctors can bring to the business, the American Society for Reproductive Medicine has set forth a number of guidelines to which many reputable doctors now adhere.[10] These guidelines are an indication of the maturing of this relatively new field and an unspoken acknowledgment of its inherent problems. As the number of people seeking treatment increases, so do word-of-mouth reports about the successes, the failures, and the costs of these treatments. Since competition is fierce in the booming infertility business, strategies to compete for customers increase. Some clinics now go so far as to offer rebates to those who do not achieve a successful pregnancy.

What is hard to grasp for some women is the fertility clinic that turns them away. Advertised success rates are essential for attracting new business, and women attempting late-in-life pregnancies can lower eye-catching numbers. Therefore, some doctors refuse to consider a woman who is forty years of age or older rather than lower their take home baby rate.

Another surprise to many is the revelation that infertility is not an exclusively female problem. According to a study by the National Survey of Family Growth, 35 percent of infertility is caused by the female, 35 percent is caused by the male, 20 percent is caused by both partners, and 10 percent is unattributable.[11] Women, it appears, have achieved equality in yet another arena—infertility. Despite this seeming parity, however, most procedures are still performed primarily on women.

In an age when success is paramount and achievement is all, how does a childless woman reconcile herself with failing to achieve her fondest desire, whether because of her own medical issues or her mate's? Given her poignant need, is it any wonder that despite dismal chances for success, she readily agrees to gamble on the fertility sweepstakes?

This is a dangerous labyrinth the childless woman enters. The first step is trying to get pregnant the old-fashioned way. When that does not work, she heads to her ob-gyn, who does some preliminary checking on her and her husband (presuming there is a husband). If her husband's sperm is not the problem and she goes a year with no success, she is referred to a fertility *expert*. The pathway becomes a slippery slope. She must choose between doctors offering Clomid, IVF, GIFT, ZIFT,[12] and a variety of other emotionally (and financially) costly procedures. The miracle drugs disorient her physically *and* emotionally.

Another year may elapse. If nothing is working, she begins to feel claustrophobic and lonely. She ventures into unknown (experimental) territory. But she can hear a baby crying, so she continues. When she comes to the end of the maze, she discovers there is no child after all, only a fantasy sound emanating from inside her desperately needy heart.

Far too often, another year or two later, the woman asks to start over. This time, she promises the doctors she will try harder and longer, until she reaches that baby she knows is waiting for her.

After many years, she finally drags herself out of the maze, too disoriented to know she needs to stop. Although her body is failing, she pushes to continue. New paths (new cures) have come along since she first began. She is convinced they will lead to her desired goal. Ignoring logic, she begs to follow another new pathway.

To someone who has never gone through what Donna, the woman in Minnesota preparing to "bury" the child she never bore, experienced, the maze scenario may sound overly dramatic. But it is not. If anything, it is a pale imitation of the actual torment infertile women go through.

Eventually, every woman who has been on the infertility road comes to the moment when she knows she must stop. Sometimes she decides herself; often others who care about her (husband, doctors, parents, friends) tell her it's time to quit.

Sally is my neighbor. She walks her beloved dog, Cooper, in front of our house and we wave to one another through the front window as our dogs bark eager greetings. Sally is bright, energetic, and cheerful. Her manner is straightforward. Her interest in my young daughter has always been genuine, and I have been touched by it. I asked her one day why she did not have children of her own. She told me she could not.

Sally spent seven years trying to have a baby. The lengths to which she went are staggering. Among them: She took Clomid, had numerous surgeries, had at least ten artificial inseminations while she and her husband lived in Florida, and then later, when they moved to Los Angeles, there were more inseminations, three in vitros, and a zygote procedure.

"Each procedure cost between $10,000 and $15,000 a pop and that was driven by how many drugs, and what combination of drugs, they required me to take," says Sally. "I was having injections every day up until the time of ovulation. . . . Bob was . . . giving me a shot every night." She shakes her blond curls, remembering those dark days. "My rear end looked like a road map . . . you know, you're beat up. And the drugs make you [feel] like you're pregnant, so your breasts are tender and your abdomen swells out. You get bloated. You have all these physical things that happen . . . and then the rest of the cycle you're getting injections of Lupron in your stomach."

In addition to the home injections, Sally visited the doctor's office every other day for blood tests and ultrasounds. Because her body was hyperstimulated, it required careful monitoring. Bob and Sally's entire lives were geared to their goal of having a baby.

"You're trying to be up and you're also conducting yourself physically and . . . nutritionally as if you're pregnant because you hope you're going to be and obviously you trust medical science or why would you be throwing $10,000 to $15,000 a month at it?" she asserts. "So you're not drinking, you're not smoking, you're not doing [any] strenuous activity. You're trying to stay calm and happy." Her eyes stray toward her living room window. "And no matter what you do, once a month . . . you're devastated." She turns back to me. "And it doesn't matter how good the rest of your life is; it doesn't matter that I have a beautiful home and a loving husband and wonderful things. Once a month, I'm so depressed and disappointed and there's no solace."

I ask what finally made her stop.

A combination of just not getting pregnant and being depressed. I got . . . morose. So I called my family doctor and said, "Marc, I'm worried about me. I feel suicidal. I am despondent beyond belief," and he said, "You've got to quit the drugs. You need to totally quit from your procedures, you need to stay away from the hormones . . . if you'll just get off of everything and move away from this a little bit, you'll come back together. All the jagged edges will fall into place." And I said, "Okay, what do I do now? Do I adopt, do I do foster care, where do I go?" And he said, "You're such a wreck you're in no position to make a major life decision."

Sally wisely did as her doctor suggested; she allowed herself to heal and made no immediate decisions.

And I've got to tell you, at that moment, it was like a reprieve. It was such a relief that . . . I didn't have to know anything. He said, "For a minimum six months, I don't want you to go there." It was like an instant life pill. And after six months I wasn't ready to think about it. It was such a damaging thing and the further I got from it, the better I felt. And now I'm forty-six and we haven't done anything.

Donna and her husband also tried numerous procedures. She had tubular surgery and spent one year attempting inseminations with no luck. Along the way, their insurance company changed, and the good news was that the new policy would cover the cost of three IVFs. Ironically, after the first IVF failed, the couple became pregnant on their own. When Donna miscarried early on, they became even more determined to continue treatments. As she prepared for the last IVF, Donna decided to take a leave of absence. "I knew if it didn't work I was going to need some time to recover." Her instincts were right. The last in vitro was a failure.

"It was devastating," Donna recalls. " The other times I told myself, well, there's always one more try." She pauses as she thinks back. "We both were home when the call came. I sobbed. It was the lowest point in my life. At the time I thought, if I can't have children, there's no reason to live."

"The worst was after the GIFT procedure didn't work," Nancy told me. (In a GIFT procedure, mature eggs and sperm are transferred to the fallopian tube, where fertilization can take place.) "Getting the call [that it did not work] was the most devastating thing. There I was, at my desk at work, and I got the call and had a meeting in ten minutes. I went into a bathroom stall and cried." Her insurance company paid for part of the surgery because it included a laparoscopy (a surgical procedure used to evaluate pelvic pathology). Even with partial coverage, GIFT cost the couple $4,500.

Infertility care is now covered by most insurance companies, but all have strict policies on the specifics of what is, and is not, included. Many of the women in this section had some infertility work covered, but each ultimately had to rely on her own financial resources to carry the burden of cost. At some point, all the woman cited a grave concern for the financial drain and questioned continuing their treatments.

"We debated about where to go from here," says Nancy. "We could scrape together the $7,500 or we could get a loan." Nancy and her husband also considered another issue when facing another GIFT procedure: "It *could* make us happy *or* take us down the toilet." Nancy and her husband weighed their options and made a decision that for them was the right one: "We took the money and bought a house. Once I stopped the drugs, I felt the burden was lifted and we were on another path."

Nancy was only thirty-two when her GIFT procedure failed. She has what is called unexplained infertility. Despite all the tests conducted on her and her husband, no doctor can tell them why they have no children. Seven years later, they are still childless.

Celia also has unexplained infertility: "I worked with two different doctors . . . [who] couldn't figure out what was wrong. They were looking for anything . . . grasping at straws. After eight years, I finally said, I can't do this anymore." She sighs as she relates her story. "One day, I found myself crying at work and that was awful. Work is work and personal is personal." Celia tried to be stoic, but it was hard. Eventually, she decided to stop treatments. Having a mother who had breast cancer caused Celia to worry about the drugs she had taken. Indeed, little is said about the long-term effect hormonal drugs may have on women who try anything to conceive.

Although many female patients with fertility problems are willing to accept donated eggs with the hope of producing a child, their husbands often are not. Marrs noted that if the problem is discovered to be due to male infertility, many husbands will opt out rather than accept donated sperm.

First, Do No Harm

Liz Tilberis, former editor in chief of *Harper's Bazaar*, chronicled her battle with cancer in her biography, *No Time to Die*.[13] While in her thirties, Tilberis underwent nine cycles of in vitro fertilization, which included hormone-stimulating medications. She was convinced her illness was the result of the fertility drugs.

A year before Tilberis's cancer was diagnosed, Dr. Alice Whittemore of Stanford University discovered that women treated with fertility drugs who later went on to have children were three times more likely to develop ovarian cancer than those who did not take the drugs. More astonishing is that women who did not succeed in achieving a pregnancy were twenty-seven times more likely to develop the disease.

"Even if they'd told me I would suffer from cancer later, I wanted a baby so desperately that I'd certainly have over-done them," says Tilberis. "But at least I'd have the knowl-edge in the back of my mind that I was at risk for ovarian cancer, so that I'd have gone for checkups and kept an eye on the situation."

Like many women, Liz Tilberis wanted children desper-ately and would try anything to have them. For her, "Being told I had cancer was not as hard as being told I was infer-tile."[14] Sadly, Tilberis lost her battle with cancer and died in 1999.

The Kindness of Strangers

Women who gamble on the infertility lottery and lose form an exclusive sorority. Bonded by a common experience and needing the support they can only get from one another, they often reach out and connect in cyberspace on one of the many Web sites devoted to women who are tragically childless. This posting appeared sometime after Mother's Day:

> Can you imagine being barely resolved to the fact that treat-ments are not going to work and then attending a church ser-vice in which all the mothers are asked to stand up and be ap-plauded . . . or attending a luncheon at which it is assumed that all women present are mothers and roses are passed out for Mother's Day? What do we do? Give the rose back?

Another woman told of attending a Yankees spring training game with her husband. She eagerly looked forward to the event:

> When we got out of the car and began to walk to the stands, there was this old couple, about in their 70s, walking hand in hand in front of us. They were walking with what looked like their adult children. Don't ask me why but suddenly it was like I was hit with a sledgehammer. I saw my dh [dear husband] and I the same age as them, walking hand in hand like them, but with no children to share it with. That is IF we are lucky enough to still have each other by that age. I suddenly felt very alone. My mind was whirling with how parents will die off and nieces and nephews go their separate ways with their own immediate families. My chest began to feel very heavy as I held back tears that were trying to burst their way out. Of course as we continued to walk, there were dads all around us taking their young sons to see the baseball game. I couldn't bear the pain of the loss of the experience that all these people were able to have and not me.

These Web sites provide many women the only opportunity they have had to share their grief.

Imagine living on a block where every house is filled with kids. All your coworkers have kids. Your sister has kids; your aunts, your cousins, and even your best friends have kids. So, who do you talk to about being infertile? On the Internet, infertile women found others in the exact same position. Some women further along in the healing process offered guidelines and support to newcomers and recommendations on how to handle awkward situations. These women were not childless by choice but by chance, not volunteers in the childless army but draftees.

"Why Don't You Adopt?"

One common problem childless women seem to encounter is the stranger who wants to offer advice: have more sex, have less sex, quit thinking about it, stop trying so hard, try another expert, try another procedure. Or finally, they urge you to adopt. Should you resist any of the above suggestions, you are judged as someone who does not really want a child.

RESOLVE, a support group for infertile couples, believes that anyone who wants a child can have one. Their philosophy is if you can't have a biological child, simply adopt (as though adoption were a simple matter). There is validity to RESOLVE's argument, considering the world's population and the number of unwanted children, yet it dismisses the needs of those who wish to have a child who is connected to them genetically.

But must a woman prove her desire to have a child by adopting?

Women who resist this challenge to adopt often bring up the following issues: doubts about the child's health, the country of origin, or the people handling the adoption; a lack of medical information available about the child; and the possibility of legal complications down the line. They worry about what will happen if the birth mother reneges or U.S. immigration officials veto the acceptance of a foreign child. They express concerns about legal snafus that could allow the birth parents to show up two or three years later and snatch a beloved child back. What then? How does one recover at that late date? They wonder about the financial burden an adoption places on a couple whose resources are already depleted from years of fertility work.

It is clear from those I spoke with that each thought long and hard about adopting as an option. Yet many feel the need to have a child connected to them genetically. "That's from my side of the family," we will hear a parent say, or, "She gets that from her grandfather." People cannot be blamed for wanting what is comfortable. A biological child, on some level at least, is comfortable.

I asked Sally about adopting. She sat back in a beautiful leather chair considering the question: "The adoption thing. When Bob and I decided to have a baby and everything was possible, I wanted to *carry* a baby. I wanted to be pregnant because Bob is adopted and he knows nothing about being related to somebody or the genetics of it; I really wanted him to have the experience of seeing his own child." Interestingly, Sally's husband Bob has a wonderful set of caring parents to whom he is devoted. His is a happy adoption scenario. Yet Sally and Bob both wanted a child of their own: "I don't want to have a baby just to have a baby . . . I wanted *our* baby. . . . But if I couldn't have our baby . . ." She pauses and shrugs. "That doesn't accomplish everything I wanted to accomplish."

Donna felt the same way: "In therapy, I realized how much I wanted my child with my husband . . . one that looked like me and Tom. I had to face that loss."

Paule had this to say: "Adoption answers the need for parenting, but it doesn't resolve the issue of pregnancy. We wanted the experience of the pregnancy *and* the child."

Paule tells of a friend who recently adopted a Korean child. Happy though the baby has made her, "she still feels the loss of not having a pregnancy."

Nancy's decision came after meeting a couple who seem to have had the most horrific adoption story ever. As she tells it:

We thought, maybe we should adopt. We did some preliminary checking. We had some concerns, health being one. That's when I realized I wanted the genetic link. Some time later, we went to a wedding and met a couple who'd adopted older kids. They had two boys and a girl and it [the adoption] was a disaster from the start. The birth mother would turn up every now and then and try and get the kids back. The adoptive daughter accused the husband of sexual molestation. . . . It nearly ruined their lives and careers. She [the wife] was suicidal. After hearing this we went, "Oh my God, to go through this and wind up like that!" The girl [who was] pregnant, ran away from home with some older boy, and went back to her mother. The youngest was shoplifting. . . . It was a wake-up call for us. . . . We said no. It's been a year now and I'm comfortable with the decision.

"Two friends adopted," Donna told me. The first couple she mentioned were ready to pick up their child (who was only a few days old) when they got a call informing them that the birth mother had "changed her mind." The second couple "had a woman in New York choose them," says Donna. "They sent her money for rent, doctor bills, et cetera. She changed her mind right before the baby was born. They then found a baby in Florida. They spent one to two weeks in Florida before the baby was born, went through the delivery with her, and took the baby home from the hospital. They had the baby three days and then the birth mother changed her mind."

Both Nancy and Donna had firsthand encounters that discouraged any thoughts they may have had about adopting. Other women cited concerns about relatives who might not fully welcome an adopted child into the family. Patty summed up the feelings of a few when she said,

> I was certain my in-laws wouldn't have accepted an adopted child. My sister-in-law [married to her husband's brother] pointed out that they don't treat her kids the same way they do their daughter's. I realized she was right. If her kids were second-class citizens, our adopted child would have been treated like a third-class citizen and that wouldn't have been right.

Others talked about the expense. Donna said, "When I spoke to people at work about adoption, they were shocked at how much it cost and how much you had to go through." Nancy talked to a couple who'd adopted during the fifties. Their adoption cost a whopping $500. She says, "All the info we had was how expensive, time consuming it was, et cetera. It's like a second job."

Couples who have been through long-term fertility work may not be in the best emotional state to take the leap of faith adopting demands. Certainly, most adoptions are successful. But people who have been on an emotional roller coaster may not be capable of handling yet another enormous risk. It is also possible that these couples were more sensitive to the negative tales about adoptions they were hearing due to what they had just been through. Whatever the reason, these experiences did act as a deterrent to their adopting a child.

Ambivalence toward adopting sometimes comes from a woman's husband. When Celia stopped infertility treatments, she talked about adopting. But her husband was reluctant: "I wanted to adopt, but every time I opened the door he slammed it shut. I went into therapy and finally [we] talked about it."

What she learned from her husband in those sessions surprised her. "When I didn't get pregnant, he was as upset as I was but didn't want to upset me more [by talking about it]. He told me, 'When it came to adoption and you didn't go through that door, I didn't think you were committed [to it].'" Finally able to talk about their situation openly, they chose *together* not to adopt.

At first Paule's husband was against the idea of adopting, but seeing her unhappiness, he yielded. Although they ultimately chose not to adopt, it became a mutual decision. "That was the biggest gift he could have given me. I will never get over my gratitude that *I* got to make the choice. I made the decision."

Patty said, "We thought about adopting from China, but it's so difficult and so expensive. We decided it was not what we wanted. I was tired of people making decisions that affected my life. During infertility treatments, we had to deal with insurance companies and doctors. I wanted to be able to decide what happened to me without having to beg others for help."

Making the decision not to adopt is the final letting go. Lori posted this on the Internet:

> I think that myself and all of you women here [on the Childfree by Chance line] are healthier in mind and soul for choosing a childfree lifestyle over adoption. Don't get me wrong, I think that ANY woman is STRONG for having gone through infertility, no matter how it ends up. But somehow women who face a childfree life have to "let go" of something that is VERY difficult to let go of. It takes a lot of courage and self-awareness to make this decision.

Faced with the reality that a baby will never be part of their lives, many women have a rough time adjusting. "I put on forty pounds," Nancy admits. A previously health-conscious individual, she now felt that "it didn't matter. I wasn't going to be a mother. There was no one depending on me." Nancy's failure to achieve her dream left her angry and sad. "Suddenly there were no long-term goals: weddings, graduations." She used food to comfort herself.

All of the women suffered varying bouts of depression. And each made the decision to move on. "At some point, it becomes a choice," Sally told me. "My God, I have so many things to be grateful for. . . . I've waited all my life to meet this fabulous man, the answer to my dreams, I was finally there and I'm destroying it." She leans toward me. "Today is mine and tomorrow is *absolutely* mine and not every experience in life is bright and cheerful and happy." She sits back and reflects.

> But if it's a dark thread running through the canvas of your life, it just adds depth and color and vibrancy. . . . They add to the richness of your life and all of that adds to a more interesting person and I can bring myself to this point and say this is who I am and these experiences just give me more reference and more to offer going forward.

One day Donna said to Tom, "'I don't want to look back on our lives and see only sadness over not having a child.' We both decided, let's get on with our lives."

"I used to think that I was being punished by God," Patty claimed. "I no longer feel that way. I'm not sure why He prevented me from having children, but maybe there is something in the future that I am destined to do."

She continued, "Nine years is a long time to be unhappy. I'm not sure if a child could have lived up to my dreamed expectations after that long a time. I thought a child would make me happy. I found that only I could make myself happy. I thought a child would make my life perfect. I think that's a lot of pressure to put on a person."

Nancy eventually came to this: "I'm important, my health is important. Enough self-pity and grieving. Just because I don't have kids doesn't mean I'm not important."

When these women came out the other side of their depression, they began to recognize some positive things about childlessness.

Patty said, "My sister-in-law told me she didn't realize how much work parenting was going to be. I hadn't thought about what it was like. I think I glamorized motherhood."

A turning point for Patty came the first time she was able to see motherhood in a realistic light:

It took about six months of talking to the CBC [Childless by Chance Internet group] before I started to come to peace with my situation. I actually decorated my house for Christmas last year. I couldn't do this the two previous years. The year before, my husband and I went driving through the subdivision and I cried while I looked at all of the decorated homes and thinking what a perfect life they must be leading with their children.

In 1997, I went out and bought new decorations and had the best-looking tree ever. I used to dream of decorating the house with the kids. My sister-in-law has to send her kids to grandma's because she can't get anything done, and then she has to yell at them to keep their hands off of everything. It doesn't sound like what I pictured.

It was not Patty's desire for a perfectly decorated Christmas tree that mattered, it was her ability to finally appreciate what she had—to see the glass as half full instead of half empty. When asked about her life now, Patty says, "I share a very close relationship with my husband. We both feel that our marriage is stronger since there is just the two of us. We have more time for travel, hobbies, and things that interest us. I realize this sounds selfish, but I feel that after nine years of infertility, I am entitled to these things."

She also spoke about her greater self-awareness:

> I think many people do not even think about having children, they just do it. . . . In the last fifteen months, I have stepped back and looked at why I wanted children. I wanted children for selfish reasons and that is not right. I wanted a child to complete my life and make it perfect. That would not have happened. So, am I selfish? The answer is, not anymore.

Celia found a different parenting role: "All our nieces, nephews, and godchildren have been important in our lives. I suddenly realized we already have children. A woman I know . . . told me, 'Never underestimate the influence you can have on a child precisely because you are *not* their parents.'"

Sally expressed the same idea a little differently: "We don't resent other people who have that happiness [children]. We both have a lot to share and a lot to give. And we take a lot of joy in mentoring . . . we're in a position where we can do things for friends and for their kids. And we do that. We get a lot of joy out of that."

These women have all moved on, but to different degrees and at their own pace. They all agree they will never get over their loss, they will only adjust to it.

"I don't think we'll ever be at peace," Sally said. "We were on a plane coming back from New York and I was right behind a women and she had a six-month-old little girl and her husband . . . they were the most beautiful mommy, daddy, baby thing I've ever seen." She pauses before she continues. "We were tender for a couple days. Just like you had surgery and you ripped something loose and you had to heal again."

In *Motherhood Deferred*, Anne Taylor Fleming, a former columnist for the *New York Times*, relates her infertility journey and the subsequent pain of coping with childlessness:

I did not heal as fast as I had hoped. As the months went by and became years, I began to understand that I would never completely heal, that I would carry with me always the child I had never had—in times of sorrow, in times of exuberance, in new and foreign places when I wanted that specific someone to show things to. That daughter. Some days I let go of it. But some days I saw her everywhere.[15]

The Big Question

Celia said, "When someone asks, 'Do you have children?' they do not want to go into the real discussion. There is so little sensitivity. There's little genuine caring about the whys and wherefores."

"I think as we got further and further along with our fertility treatments, we started to withdraw from friends," Donna shared,

> as well as they started drawing away from us. They were going along with their lives, having children while we weren't. It seemed with a lot of them, they didn't know what to say or do, so they didn't say anything! If *we* didn't reach out to them, there was no contact. That's been a painful realization for me, with family and friends. We've suffered this pain, a lot of it, on our own. Infertility isn't as obvious as a death and loss of a loved one, although I think it's as painful. Yet we haven't gotten the acknowledgment, sympathy, or empathy, et cetera., that people do from a death loss.

So Donna will mourn her loss in private. And when she is ready, she will bury her dreams in her own backyard.

HAPPENSTANCE

When you make the world tolerable for yourself, you make the world tolerable for others.

—Anaïs Nin[1]

3

Happenstance

Some things in life just happen. You can be dragged by a friend to a party you did *not* want to go to and meet the man of your dreams. You may take a job offer in a town you weren't sure you wanted to transfer to and discover your ideal community. With each turn, your life changes course.

How much easier things would be if flashing neon lights pointed the way to our future. Rather, we are left to discover our path in fits and starts. We take one step forward (e.g., get married or go to school), then take two steps back (quit a job, get divorced) before we each find our true place in life. The business we pursue, where we wind up going to school, who becomes our best friend—all these important decisions take time to develop. Even who a woman marries is an involved process. We meet, we date, we fall in love and *then* decide to take the plunge.

Careers are often no different. We may begin in one line of work, but discover along the way that our wants, our talents, and our limitations are not suited to our first choice. Conversely, we can find ourselves more enriched and challenged by our work than we ever thought possible. In both instances, we are surprised by our discoveries.

So it is with plans for mothering. Although most of the women in this section thought they would one day parent, they have nonetheless remained childless. For them, the road to childlessness was an evolutionary journey—one they did not expect to take.

Women who are childless by childhood had upbringings that nullified their desire for mothering because of the parenting they did—or did not—receive. They may discover their mothering needs when it is too late to conceive.

Some women are reared with a set of values that dictate they be married before they have children. Since the right man does not come along, they never mother. They are childless by standards.

These days, many women marry older men. Many of these men are divorced fathers who do not wish to begin parenting again late in life. Their wives become childless by marriage.

A great many women find their lives so fulfilling, their careers so engrossing, there is simply no need for a child. Although they always expected they would one day mother, they do not. They are unexpectedly childless.

These various and compelling reasons led the women in this section to be childless by happenstance.

Childless by Childhood

Of all the jobs one takes on in life, none has more impact on another's life than parenting. People often embark on parenting without the skills, and sometimes even without the desire, to do the kind of job that is required.

Parents teach children every day. Although parents prefer children follow the verbal lessons they offer, it is from example that we learn most. When messages are delivered by parents who are themselves damaged, the child becomes the unwitting recipient of injurious, and often life-altering, information.

Children are soul readers. Whether or not parents acknowledge it, children feel deeply—but may not have the capacities yet to be fully aware. In his seminal work on child development, Erik Erikson writes: "Children tend to sense the unconscious insecurities and intentions as well as the conscious thoughts and overt behavior of their parents, even though they do not understand their cause and meaning."[2] In other words, kids know what the emotional score is. A look, a frown, a stare—whether directed at the child or not—speaks volumes. Parents therefore are responsible not only for how their behavior affects them but how it affects their child.

Most parents want to believe that simply loving a child is all that is needed to be a good parent. But children need more than just love. Love, after all, runs the gamut from obsession (unhealthy love) to adoration (the goal). At heart, children want to know they are a joy in their parents' lives;

they wish to be a vital part of the family structure; and they need to feel safe.

It would seem that children intuit almost from birth. Even at a preverbal level, they decipher what they see around them and translate this knowledge into their own emotional data bank. With good messages, children do well in life. Given bad messages, children make false assumptions.

It is no wonder then that the messages some women receive during childhood contribute to their eliminating parenting as a choice. So rooted are the negative lessons these women learn about mothering that it sometimes takes years to unearth them—years during which their own childbearing would take place.

Learning by Example

Valerie was raised in New York City. When her parents met, her father was a successful actor and her mother an up-and-coming painter. They were two talented artists with active careers. Watching the compromises her mother and father made in their respective professions, simply because they were parents, affected Valerie deeply.

When Valerie's mother died, she and her sister went through her personal effects. Among them was a letter from an older friend to her mother congratulating her on her engagement. Valerie unfolded the fading letter and read, "You have an enormous gift and an enormous talent and I hope in marrying that you will take that into account when you think about having children."

Her mother ignored her friend's admonition:

> I witnessed my mother, an astonishingly gifted artist, manage
> to care for a husband—freeing him up to pursue his career, his
> passion—three children, a dog, and a house with such loving
> completeness and drag her paints up from the basement every
> day because that's where the light was and then schlep them
> back downstairs before the return of the Mongolian hordes—
> i.e., her loved ones.

Her mother made her choice, a popular one at the time,
which perhaps she would defend today—but her children's
keen sense of observation told them something else. "My
mother never realized the artist she really was or might
have become . . . and never knew what place she might
have held in the world of her peers."

Valerie speaks with a passion she undoubtedly inherited
from her parents. Her living room, however, is a study in
tranquillity. As she talks, her coffee cup punctuates the air
for emphasis. She sits framed by a large picture window
facing out on a secluded, lush garden. On the walls, mas-
sive paintings splashed with bold colors add texture to the
room. From her mother, Valerie inherited an appreciation
of art. Warm, intelligent eyes, set in a face caressed by
swinging auburn hair, reinforce the intensity of her story-
telling. She remembers watching her mother paint:

> Fast Daumier-like sketches of the priest and the altar boy at the
> Communion rail, freezing a dead bird for future [still-life]

study, night classes in Chinese water color . . . were all caught on the fly because she had children she loved and wanted to do right by. And we loved her and in loving her we couldn't help but feel the deep pocket of her pain, her loss. So this is the equation I made back then: Children equals sacrifice.

Valerie eases back in her chair. "And even knowing I was growing up in another generation where that sacrifice was no longer expected, not even the norm, it was still a concept hard to shake."

The Great Wait

Valerie did not know she was the recipient of any negative message that would cause her to wind up childless. As she told me: "It wasn't a question of not having children at all, but of waiting. Waiting for the career to secure itself, waiting for the right man at the right time, waiting for all of those illusory expectations to materialize. And then I'd see."

But the message Valerie did take in was clear: If you wanted to work, you could not have children. Her decision, gleaned by watching her mother's experience, was reinforced by her father's journey.

"When radio sort of died, he [my father] thought it was just a passing thing. He thought radio would be back. When he realized he didn't have a career, he was afraid to start over." Her coffee cup is empty and she places it gently on the table. She leans in: "He had a responsibility to three children, so he gave up acting . . . and I saw him die a little bit every day after that. . . . [My parents] kept their pain private, but children are very sensitive and aware. . . . It was a huge burden to feel my parents' individual and collective pain, and I associated it with having children."

The noted child developmentalist Bruno Bettelheim explains, "While, physiologically speaking, the parent creates the child, it is the arrival of the child which causes the parental problem, and with these come his own."[3]

From early childhood, Valerie's own artistic leanings were applauded and encouraged by her parents. Strangely, there was never a word of caution about combining family life and artistic goals. But there didn't need to be. Although her parents quietly accepted their situation, she recognized what it had cost them and was loath to repeat it.

If Valerie's parents could be interviewed, they might speak eloquently about the happiness parenting brought them. Indeed, they may have made the perfect choices for themselves. Or perhaps they would confirm the unspoken truth that Valerie observed. What matters is how she interpreted it.

And it has left Valerie with some mixed feelings about her childlessness:

I know I was so sensitive to information I was given [as a child], I misapplied it and I'm sorry about that and I didn't realize until it was too late. And so all the advice I gave myself in terms of not having children (that I had a career, that I had ambition, that I was too selfish to do it)—all those things that I did so resolutely . . . I didn't allow myself room for something other than what I had been exposed to . . . I ill-advised myself, for whatever reasons.

All children make some erroneous assumptions based on parental messages during their growing up. So deeply rooted are these ideas that often they are not uncovered until we are quite grown up ourselves. For women, whose childbearing years are limited, these revelations sometimes come too late.

Fear of Trying

Unlike the situation with Valerie, whose parents' difficulties stemmed from artistic frustrations, Judith's parents' problems were self-perpetuating. Reared outside of Chicago with an alcoholic father and a narcissistic mother, Judith felt completely alienated from her parents. Highly social creatures who entertained and partied on a regular basis, her parents spent scant time with their three daughters. Judith explains:

My parents argued constantly. We lived in a highly charged atmosphere, and my mother's unpredictability, along with my father's drunken rages, added to the mix. As children, my sisters and I were left to fend for ourselves. It took growing up and seeing how healthy families operate to recognize how tragic our whole upbringing was. I honestly don't remember my mother telling me she loved me until I was an adult. In fact, when my mother did mother me, in the traditional sense of the word, it felt strange.

Not only did Judith get the subliminal message that she was marginal in her mother's life, she also had no one to counterbalance these signals. As any child of an alcoholic knows, an alcoholic parent is unreliable. Without a stable father to balance her mother's erraticism, Judith was set adrift. It is not surprising that she and her sisters are close to this day. Their shared experience of a traumatic childhood welded their bond.

"Only when I turned sixteen did my mother start to relate to me," Judith chuckles. "And I think that was because she could finally socialize with me."

Judith decided marriage was not for her. She did not even think as far as having children. "I wasn't going to have a relationship, period. It was just too scary."

Damage perpetrated in childhood is far-reaching. In their 1997 work *Children of Alcoholics and Adolescence*, Tony Crespi and Ronald Sabatelli conclude that "many children of alcoholics bring from their family of origin ways of coping that may interfere with their ability to form a mature identity and capacity for intimacy."[4] It has been reported that "adults who grew up with an alcoholic parent are a third more likely to end up divorced. Part of the reason may lie in the depression and self-esteem problems that often plague the progeny of heavy drinkers. But a new study suggests that living with alcoholic parents also poisons kids' view of marriage—predisposing their own relationships to fail."5

Judith agrees. "That's probably why it was so hard for me to trust my relationship with Joao when we first met. I didn't expect it to last and was shocked when it not only continued, but grew stronger. We'd both been rather damaged by our childhoods, [and] it took years before either of us was ready to marry. But once we did, our relationship only got better."

Luckily for her, Judith found her perfect mate, someone who understood and empathized with her. Together, they worked hard at establishing a healthy, supportive relationship and defied the fate that statistically befalls many children of alcoholics.

Eventually, some of Judith's wounds began to heal. "By the time we'd been together ten years, I sensed a shift in myself emotionally. I began to trust that our marriage would not only last, it would probably get even better."

At this stage, Judith had enough life experience (and some therapy) to reformulate her feelings. When that occurred, something opened up inside her.

"Though I'd never felt a mothering instinct before, suddenly I did. I think it was not only fear that had kept my desires for a baby numbed within me for so many years, but also a feeling of unworthiness." She gives an ironic smile. "So there I was at age thirty-eight, melting at the sight of babies.

"We began fertility treatments right away, which went on for three years with no results. Finally, I had surgery, which revealed the nature of the problem." Judith's voice drops into a deeper register, and her brow tightens. "The news was bad. One fallopian tube was badly twisted and scarred, the other completely destroyed. The doctor gave us a 6 to 8 percent chance for conception. We were devastated. I began to lose heart in the whole endeavor. The odds were just too overwhelming. It was too costly a gamble . . . financially and emotionally."

For someone like Judith, discovering her mothering needs and having them rendered impossible was a cruel twist of fate.

"I think back and wonder . . . perhaps if I'd been raised in a normal atmosphere, or even a semi-normal atmosphere, it wouldn't have taken me so long to get around to wanting a child. But that's not what happened." Her hands turn upward. "I was and here I am." Judith's mother had no intention when she became a parent to do damage to any of her children. Yet she did.

Where Is the Love?

Phoebe is a sixty-two-year-old woman who is convinced her mother did not love her: "She was so narcissistic that there never was a child involved, there was only the mother. There were never birthday cards for the children, but there were always Mother's Day cards." Like Judith,

Phoebe discovered her mothering instincts when it was too late to act on them. Phoebe told her therapist that she could not conceive of a mother not loving her child. The doctor then shared with her some startling news: that she had patients who did not love their children. The doctor's revelation helped Phoebe heal. Before, Phoebe had always felt that being childless was unnatural. "Being childless isn't an aberration; being a mother who hates her child, now *that's* an aberration."

"I Won't Go Home Again"

Examining childhood is difficult for many individuals. Some bury the memories of youth in an emotional vault, grateful they no longer experience pain. To avoid rekindling those memories, some women will go so far as not to have children rather than risk the feelings they might possibly be unlocking.

Eva tells me: "My childhood was difficult. And the thought of reliving that, I just didn't want to do. I was afraid of imposing [on a child] things from my [own] childhood."

A tiny woman, Eva sits cross-legged in a chair, taut like a spring. Even her curly hair and lively eyes give the feeling she might bounce up at any moment. Her hands, which seem to reinforce her thoughts, are in constant motion.

"I remember being the child of parents who had a lot of stuff they needed to deal with, and I don't regret not having a child to drag through all that. My parents were 'good people' material, but they weren't parent material."

Eva's mother and father were committed union organizers and communists. As antiwar activists, they were often involved in dangerous confrontations. On more than one occasion, Eva was dragged along and watched in horror as her parents were arrested.

"It was hard to be the child of communists in the 1950s. I got beaten up, had rocks thrown at me, things like that. Being a young white child back then, drinking out of a blacks-only drinking fountain, wasn't easy. It was hard to go on civil rights demonstrations and see people's hatred." Eva stiffens in her chair and draws in a breath. "I wasn't protected the way a child should be."

Kim Williams and her husband are peace activists involved with the Prince of Peace Plowshares, a religiously affiliated group. Her husband has been jailed numerous times, which she says has been particularly hard on their young son, Daniel. "I don't relish what my child, or any child of the other Plowshares' children, are going through. I don't think it's easy on any of them."[6] Kim then goes on to say, "But I do think the situation we are in as the world's superpower [is] the cause of so much suffering and misery, requires some sort of sacrifice and that some day the young ones will understand this more clearly." Twenty years from now, it would be interesting to interview Daniel and see if his mother's prediction came true or if he, like Eva, will suffer from the abandonment and fear that overtakes a young child when a parent is suddenly wrenched away and put in jail. Idealism is the mark of those who engage in activist adventures. But it is one thing to commit oneself to a political belief and quite another to drag an unwitting child into it as well.

Eva said, "My mother believed that you don't own your children, but she took it too far."

Although Eva grew up to respect the political choices her parents made, feeling unprotected and disconnected from her mother had a damaging effect on her: "I wanted to have a child, but I was also frightened to death about what kind of mother I would be. And what that would be like for a child."

John Bowlby, a noted child development specialist, wrote, "The role of the care-giver [is] first to be available and responsive as and when wanted. Not only is it a key role but there is substantial evidence that how it is discharged by a person's parents determines in great degree whether or not he grows up to be mentally healthy."[7]

For Eva, her mother's treatment of her as just another "citizen of the world" was disconcerting. The nurturing that was Eva's due, and was needed, was unavailable. If a child cannot count on her own mother for nourishing, she must somehow provide it for herself.

"I learned to find nurturing from other people," Eva tells me. "And I learned to lower my expectations to a very low level."

No doubt some people survive horrendous childhoods relatively unscathed. Nonetheless, most of us are affected by the messages our parents send.

Valerie, Judith, and Eva have gone on to create wonderful lives for themselves. Yet each feels that something is missing—the experience of having a child. Adoption became moot because by the time each woman discovered her desire, she felt too old to begin the process. Indeed, their childlessness, they believe, is a direct result of their childhood experiences.

"I think children are straight from heaven," Eva says. She is now up and pacing the room. Earlier sadness has transformed into delight. Her voice bubbles: "They are full of love and joy. All you have to do is spend some time with them to know how sacred they are. Children teach us about the wonders of being alive."

Suddenly, Eva's mood darkens. She stops moving. "When I hear someone say they spend it [their love] on their cats, I want to slap that person." She leans over the table and with great intensity tells me, "You can't spend time with a cat and know about the miracle."

How ironic that someone with such a clear appreciation for children does not have any. When I mention this, she shakes her head. Her tone is softer now.

"Don't feel sorry for me because I don't have a child. Everything I have to offer a child, I offer."

Luckily for the children she works with on a daily basis, Eva is a woman who has made peace with herself—a peace not easily arrived at for many women.

"Right after I had my surgery I went to the movies by myself and saw *Parenthood*," Judith related. "I sobbed all the way through the ending [the birth scene]. That probably sounds like a very self-destructive thing to do, but it was a kind of purging.

"I'm almost fifty now and still can't watch a movie in which there's a birth." Her voice falters. "I know I'll get over it one day, but there's a part of me that holds out hope, even though I know it's completely unrealistic." Judith's pain is palpable. For her, the wound remains fresh.

"I finally got what a joyous experience it [parenting] can be with my friends who did it late," says Valerie. "Seeing children through my current eyes, I get how fabulous it is. But I was someplace else . . . and [now] it's just a curiosity as to what I . . . missed in life."

These three women understand just how permanent a role parents play in the life of a child because in many ways their parents cost them their children.

Childless by Standards

Mary Ann lives on a tree-lined street in a house with a white picket fence and a bright blue door. She has a yappy dog that greets visitors with high leaps and sloppy kisses. Inside the antique-filled home, hearty plants flourish and sunshine streams through lace-covered windows. The picture is perfect Norman Rockwell, a home Mary Ann created especially for a family—except she has no husband and she has no child.

Like many women over forty, Mary Ann always expected to one day marry and have children. But it never happened.

For a myriad of reasons, at age forty-six, Mary Ann is one of the 41 percent of women her age who never have a child.[8] Like many women raised during the 1950s and 1960s, Mary Ann had an upbringing shaped by many of the values she still holds sacred today. Those standards helped guide these women to become productive, caring human beings. But those same values also obfuscated any chance of fulfilling one of their childhood dreams: to become a mother.

It is painful never to meet your soul mate, the man of your dreams, your Prince Charming. It is doubly painful when your own moral code dictates that the motherhood you so deeply desire can only follow marriage.

"I would never consider having a child unless I was married," Mary Ann says. She admits that her childlessness and her singleness are very integrated.

Reared by an Italian Catholic mother who was divorced, Mary Ann remembers that in high school there were good girls (virgins) and bad girls (those who were not). "There was a subtext [back then], there were dictums, there was parental disapproval, there was even shame."

Mary Ann recalls two scandals from her childhood: The first was the birth of Isabella Rossellini to the unmarried Ingrid Bergman and Roberto Rossellini. Bergman bravely told the press, "Even if the world should fall upon me, I don't care. This is my child and I want it." Her words were strong, but as one film journalist noted, "She must have foreseen the puritanical outrage her pregnancy would incite—vilified and virtually blacklisted by the American press for her fall from grace, Bergman spent the next seven years in self-exile, appearing only in Rossellini's films—films which were largely ignored in the U.S."[9]

The second scandal involved Sophia Loren and Carlo Ponti, a married man with two children. Loren suffered through years of frustration while Ponti, a Catholic, tried to obtain an annulment from the church.

> In 1962, Ponti finally secured a divorce from his wife and a subsequent marriage by proxy to Loren in legal proceedings in Mexico. Ponti's finaglings were later rendered invalid by the Vatican, and the two were forced to live as exiles and then as secret lovers in Rome to avoid excommunication. They ultimately subverted the Vatican's pronouncements of bigamy and concubinage by becoming citizens of France and remarrying legally in 1966.[10]

Although common and less shocking today, such public scandals served as powerful lessons to impressionable young girls at the time, lessons that parents and teachers utilized to demonstrate the importance of following the "correct" path. They illustrated an uncontrovertible moral and social code.

Name Change

These days, out-of-wedlock children raise very few eyebrows. Stars think nothing of reproducing without the benefit of marriage. No one illustrates this better than the pop icon Madonna. Reared a Catholic, she is rearing her out-of-wedlock children Catholic. She remains tied to her religion, but clearly not to its precepts. Free from social maxims, these younger women are capable of fulfilling their mothering needs. But for women brought up in another era or bound by a strong personal value system, that option is impossible.

Words like "bastard" and "illegitimate" are no longer used to describe a child born to an unwed mother. They are antiquated words from a bygone era. Even the U.S. Center for Disease Control has altered its phraseology to accommodate a new consciousness regarding this issue. Out-of-wedlock children are now referred to as "nonmarital."[11] The U.S. Department of Health and Human Services now follows suit by using the term "nonmarital" to describe these births.[12]

Women like Mary Ann who grew up during the Eisenhower presidency, however, clearly recall the scorn for a girl who "got herself into trouble." To spare a family shame, unwed mothers were sometimes shipped off to a relative in another state or placed in a home for unwed mothers until the baby was born and often placed up for adoption. Since women in those days were dependent on men for financial wherewithal, not to mention social status, waiting until marriage for sex made sense. A mother's admonition to her daughter to remain a virgin carried a practical overtone as well as a social obligation.

Contraception changed the rules. Sex without consequences (at least ones with diapers) gave women sexual freedom, and going to work obliterated the need for financial support from men. In an amazingly short amount of time, the tie between morality and mothering became muddied. Fifty years ago, Mary Ann would have been a social outcast if she had had a child without a husband. Today, friends would throw her a baby shower.

A study by the University of Michigan found that the number of couples cohabiting—and having children without being married—is on the rise.[13] Mary Ann shakes her head: "Women are mating with men that they don't necessarily want as partners. It's just serial monogamy. There's no moral code." She believes the lack of commitment exemplifies a younger generation that is, at heart, selfish. "It was a lot harder to do it our way."

There does remain an injunction against some females having babies out of wedlock, but it is focused on the poor and the young. Contrary to what many believe, the increase in young mothers is not with minorities but with white women, whose rates increased tenfold from 1960 to 1992. Babies having babies is known to create a cycle of poverty that becomes nearly impossible for a young mother and her infant to escape. Knowing this, counselors, teachers, and health service workers endeavor to educate young girls about the ramifications of a pregnancy.[14] Their precept is not based on morals but on economic concerns.

Based on this value system, if a sixteen-year-old girl was suddenly handed a good deal of money, the argument against her having a baby would ostensibly evaporate (situational morality at its best). She would have the finances, if not the emotional maturity, to raise a child—a moral judgment would not be assigned to the decision.

No Absolution

Mary Ann's dilemma is not as easily rectified. No one can absolve her of her immutable moral code. She is bound by her values. Although Mary Ann wanted a child, she could never bring herself to have one without a husband.

It is difficult sometimes for today's younger women to understand why older women remain childless simply because they do not have a husband. Unless one has been reared with a strict credo, it is impossible to grasp how deeply it can affect a person's decisions. Jodie, a Gen-Xer, says, "If they want a baby so badly, why don't they just have one? What's the big deal?"

Rather than being admired for retaining the high standards she was raised with, Mary Ann is often derided for them. Over dinner recently with a colleague she barely knew, Mary Ann casually asked if he knew any eligible men. He said he was surprised she was still looking. "What's the big deal . . . you've been married." When Mary Ann admitted she hadn't, his comment was, "Well, what's wrong with you, girl?"

Kate, forty-three, has heard the same response, especially from men. A statuesque redhead who has never wanted for male companionship, Kate observed: "If I'd say I've been married four times—and I failed at each marriage—that would be fine, that would be normal." But *never* to have married is not. She shakes her head. "People think there's something wrong with you if no one has ever asked you."

"When did I get to be a bad person because I never married?" Mary Ann wants to know. "How did that happen? Because I was bright enough to walk away from a couple of guys who were pretty good catches—but in hindsight my instincts were absolutely right—it wouldn't have been a good marriage. When did I get to be damaged goods?"

Mary Ann talks about the married women she knows who develop a certain smugness. "They think they've got it down, they've got it wrapped. And I'm thinking, all you did was say 'yes' to somebody. I saw what it does to somebody when it's not okay. I want it *right*."

Her principles have nonetheless left her alone and occasionally the object of pity. She tells about the young mothers who work for her, of whom she is very fond, and for whom she acts as a surrogate mother:

I think the kids that work for me feel sorry for me. And they do, because they care for me. I keep hoping that while I'm out at the theater, or at a museum, I might run into a distinguished gentleman who wants to spend the rest of his life with me and then I can [take care of] his grandchildren. At least then someone will call me something. That's probably the hardest. Nobody's ever going to call me mom . . . ever.

Kate is seated behind an oversized blond desk in her private office, framed by a huge window looking out her Century City office in Los Angeles. She, too, hears the whispers around her office. "They look at me and say, 'I do *not* want to become you. I do not want to be lonely at forty and only have a career.'"

She senses a difference with today's young working women. She believes they have learned from watching her generation. At lunch one day, she overheard a young woman vehemently tell a friend, "I am *not* going to be one of those women who doesn't have a child until she's forty!" The young woman implied her single life and childlessness were a matter of choice for Kate.

Mary Ann and Kate are told they are too picky, their standards are impossible, and they should adopt. They are rebuked as being solely responsible for their dilemma. The admonishments are relentless—and isolating. They have learned not to speak about their pain rather than face another lecture. Mary Ann says, "You go on, you do the best you can. I have a very successful career [but] I would walk out of the door tomorrow in exchange for the things I would like. Nobody believes me . . . so I'm being penalized for doing a good job of coping."

Kate admits, "I want to have it all. Look at the age I am and I'm still fantasizing that I'm gonna meet a wealthy guy who's gonna have children of his own from a previous life maybe and I'm gonna get to live the [life of a] princess. I'm gonna get to have a career, have a guy with money, have children. I still have that fantasy."

The Adoption Option

When asked why she chose not to adopt, Mary Ann says being the product of divorce, watching her single mother cope, taught her a lesson. The child suffers and she did not want a child to experience what she had while growing up. "I missed having a dad. That was hard on me."

Now fifty-four, Victoria seriously considered adopting a child when she was forty. Victoria sits behind a sleek desk piled high with papers in her spacious office. Although she is friendly and open, the topic is clearly painful for her. "When I was forty, I started thinking about being a single parent. And I looked into adoption. I looked into foreign adoption. I talked to a couple of people who'd done it. I decided not to because I was a workaholic. This kind of a job, there have always been sixty-, seventy-hour weeks." She turns to gaze out the window. "You cannot have a child. I did not want to be that kind of a mother. You know, give my child over to a nanny or day care." She turns back. "I couldn't do that." She smiles ruefully. "I think that was a pretty unselfish thing for me to do at the time."

When I ask if she regrets her decision, Victoria becomes reflective: "Parts of me still wishes I'd gone through with it, [but] I'd have a messed-up kid on my hands in therapy. . . . It wasn't fair."

Victoria did meet the man of her dreams, but not until she was forty-four.

"I wish I had kids, I really do. I wish I had a child or two definitely. And had I met my husband earlier, we would have had children."

Anita is forty-two and shares this perspective. She also did not want to place a child in day care: "*Couldn't* put it in day care!" she exclaims.

These shared concerns for the child these women could have had is indicative of the circumspection involved in their decision. An acute awareness of a child's needs, versus their own, plays a major role in why many women forgo children. They believe that children should be the major focus of a woman's life, that children flourish in two-parent homes, that parents need to be available to children on a consistent basis, and that they could not provide this.

Although some might consider this thinking atavistic, some experts concur. The American Psychological Association reports:

> Life in a single parent household—though common—can be quite stressful for the adult and the children. Members may unrealistically expect that the family can function like a two parent family home and may feel that something is wrong when it cannot. The single parent may feel overwhelmed by the responsibility of juggling care for the children, maintaining a job and keeping up with the bills and household chores.[15]

The boomer generation is credited with revolutionizing female roles and male-female relationships. Virginity is now quaint, marriage is optional, living together de rigueur, abortion available, and commitment transitory. Yet despite all that, for some members of the boomer generation, and subsequent generations, core values remain intact.

Recognizing that single parenthood would be too taxing and believing that children need fathers, Mary Ann, Kate, Anita, and Victoria remained loyal to their standards and did not have a child. These women display their mothering instincts by choosing what is best for the child—in this case, by not having one. This is surely a selfless act in an era that some find filled with selfishness.

Childless by Marriage

The dewy-eyed romanticism that accompanied a bride down the aisle in the 1950s has slowly been replaced by today's hyperrealistic, let's-not-take-any-chances prenuptial agreement. As divorce becomes more acceptable, the notion of a lifelong marriage seems if not an unattainable goal, at least a speculative one.

The marriage contracts of the couples in this section read: I vow to love, honor, and *not* have children. For the most part, the couples here are very intentionally childless, and it is often the husband who chooses the childless path.

Couples may well wonder if a happy marriage is anachronistic in today's world. But although marriage today may require more fortitude than our parents had to muster, there does seem to be one way to shore up a bride and groom's chances for wedded bliss: If you want a happy marriage, do not mess things up by having children. Numerous studies verify that the presence of a child in a family greatly lowers the marital happiness or satisfaction of the parents.[16]

Childless couples must be passing the word. The number of couples opting to remain just that, a couple, have skyrocketed over the past three decades. Rather than bucking the trend, childless couples may actually be setting it. The U.S. Census Bureau reports that in 1965, 43.4 percent of all married couples were childless. In 1996, that figure was 53 percent.[17]

The reasons why men remain childless are often the same as women's. Some husbands experience unhappy childhoods and do not want to place themselves in a traditional domestic situation ever again. Contemplating the notion of having kids, one interviewee told me, "You'd have to have a lot of guts to dip into our family's gene pool."

Other reasons abound: Often a man with children from a previous marriage will not wish, for financial or emotional reasons, to parent all over again. If that man is thinking about retiring in the not-too-distant future, he may not relish spending his nest egg on yet another child.

Occasionally, a man who helped raise siblings without the presence of a father in the home will feel that he has done a lifetime's worth of parenting already. He refuses to start over again when he marries. Like some women, some men know they do not possess the necessary "parenting" instinct—they are not nurturers and would resent the role.

Why, Oh, Why

Although a husband may be the driving force for childlessness in many marriages, often it is a mutual decision. And the reasons are plentiful.

Some couples choose childlessness out of financial considerations. It is not that they cannot afford a child; rather it is a choice as to how they choose to spend their combined income. In the 1980s, an acronym was coined for these couples, DINKs: double income, no kids. Not only do DINK couples have more time for the pursuit of personal pleasures (such as travel, sports, and hobbies); they also have the financial wherewithal to indulge in them. Money that otherwise would have paid for children's braces, cars, and higher education can be spent on themselves.

Another reason that many a couple remains childless is articulated in *The Future of Marriage*. The author, J. Bernard, found the childless couples he polled reported a very high degree of emotional and sexual intimacy with their partners. Ask any married couple who has children and they will confirm the obvious: Tired people who have no privacy have little time for sex. Since sexual attraction is what generally brings two people together in the first place, this strong bond is hard to relinquish.[18]

The freedom to live a self-directed life in partnership with the person you love is compelling. Researchers find one of the strongest reasons couples give for remaining childless is the unique amount of time they are allowed to spend with one another. They feel the uninterrupted intimacy they share is a gift and they would be loath to surrender the special bond they have developed.

A peaceful home life is another motivating factor for childless couples. Sleeping in on a Sunday morning, then leisurely perusing the morning paper holds a great deal of appeal to many. Small wonder previously married men with children are reluctant to trade this type of Bach-filled Sunday for the ones they survived with Nintendo blasting in the background.

Coming Around to It

Not every couple begins married life set on a childless path. For some, it is simply an evolutionary process. For working couples especially, life may reveal itself to be fulfilling as is. Although not overtly committed to childlessness, they find themselves postponing the decision until one day it is too late.

J. Veevers, a respected researcher in the area of childless couples, concludes that, for many, postponing the decision of whether or not to bear children turns into a decision never to have them.[19] Elaine Campbell, in her book *The Childless Marriage*, concurs: "Simply extended, the notion of planned parenthood includes the option—no parenthood."[20]

A Bird in the Hand

Although some enter a childless marriage committed to staying that way and others drift into the state, some individuals join only after a great deal of soul-searching on the subject. A woman whose dream has always been to have a family must think long and hard before marrying a man committed to a childfree lifestyle. Timing will be critical in her decision-making process. If she meets this man when she is in her early thirties, she may end the relationship with the hopes of meeting a child-minded partner in the future. When she reaches age forty-two, her verdict may be different.

To have a loving partner with whom she can share a life, one she may have waited years to meet, a woman may be willing to give up an opportunity at motherhood. Although not her first choice, she may see a childless marriage as a worthy trade-off. Her challenge is to make the right decision without benefit of a crystal ball.

Gailyn is thirty-nine years old and has been married for a year and a half to a man she is clearly crazy about. Her husband is a widowed father of two grown children. Gailyn accepted two things when she married David: that she was marrying an older man (her husband is twenty-one years older than she) and that she would not have children.

"I think the conscious decision not to have children was [made] when David and I were courting. . . . David at no point said, 'We're not going to have children and if you have to have children then we won't get married.' David said, 'I've raised two children, I love them, but I don't want to start all over again.'" Gailyn understood his position completely.

Gailyn's decision to renounce children, however, was not made without serious consideration. She knew she was "giving up a need, a part of myself," but she did so willingly because of the special relationship she had found with David.

What helped bolster Gailyn's decision was that she always knew she "would never have a child unless my husband wanted children just as much as I did." Since David felt that he was through with his parenting years, Gailyn's decision was in essence made for her. Although Gailyn is comfortable with her decision, she is not unaware of the complex nature of her commitment. "My husband and I really talked about it and I think he feels badly because he thinks there might be something missing for me." She admits to occasional moments of sadness. But she and David talked things through before their marriage, and whenever necessary, they still do.

Talking It Out

Dr. Margaret Rubin, a psychotherapist who regularly counsels couples facing these problems, notes: "I think couples who survive are those who take comfort from one another—couples that can talk openly about their regrets, who are willing to revisit the issue every time it comes up."

Rubin observes that in a situation of this nature, the issue is never completely resolved—it can resurface again and again. "Compromises that work are those that get re-reviewed when necessary."[21]

Compromise is a reality in any good marriage: Without a healthy give-and-take by both individuals, no marriage can flourish. But compromise is one thing; relinquishing one's dream is another. Although Gailyn may have wanted a child, it was not critical to her personal happiness. Clearly, she was willing to give up one want for a greater one—a happy marriage.

Terri always liked kids, yet knew from the minute she started dating Doc that he was vehemently antichildren and if she wanted him in her life, she would have to reconsider having children: "I knew what his feeling was on the subject, so it was more if I wanted to marry him, that would have to be my choice too. And I was kind of ambivalent. I'd never been someone who desperately wanted a child—I wanted a family—but when I met someone who I thought was right, *that* was important."

As we speak, unknown to Terri, Doc steals behind her into their kitchen, ostensibly to check a pot on the stove. He is completely silent as he lifts the lid and stirs, his head cocked to listen to his wife.

"Nothing in my life was so simple. But I just met him and, you know, everybody comes with their beliefs, their package, and that was him and that's what I was choosing. It was easy for me. I didn't have to decide. I chose. I chose my husband." Doc smiles, hearing this.

I ask if she has any regrets. "Sometimes I feel there is a little pain." One such occasion was when she accompanied a friend to her ultrasound. Seeing her friend's baby, Terri was suddenly aware of what she had sacrificed. Silent tears fall down her cheeks. In the kitchen, Doc's chin lowers to his chest. He soundlessly replaces the lid on the pot and slides out of view.

Terri said many friends worried when she and Doc became serious. They wondered what would happen if she changed her mind about having children. So far she has not. "Doc's sister has two kids, so there are kids in my life. And I'm always happy when they go away because it's exhausting and it's constant and I don't know if I have the patience."

"What's hard about being truly mature," Rubin told me, "is that we thought when we were younger that we could have it all—and nobody gets it all."

With so many women marrying later in life, mature women often approach a loving relationship with a kind of awe. To fall in love and meet your mate—especially for a woman who has been single for a long time—becomes more important than mothering. For Gailyn and Terri, the love they discovered when they found their husbands brings great fulfillment to their lives.

Terri's friends, who worry that she may someday change her mind, are not the only ones who speak out. Often families express their concern to, or even reproach, a woman who has chosen a man who does not want children. When it comes to family, the issue often becomes an emotional powder keg—and couples need to learn effective ways to defuse this bomb.

Coping with Others

Childless by Choice (CBC), the active prochildless group, was founded by a childless husband-and-wife team, Carin Smith and Jay Bender. They operate out of Leavenworth, Washington, offering advice to couples who face the everyday pressures of living in a pronatalist society: "People who can't accept your decision are likely to feel threatened by it. Instead of focusing on you and your decision, ask them why they feel so strongly that they must press their feelings on you. Focus the attention on *their* feelings instead of *your* decision. How can *their* needs be met other than by asking *you* to bear children?"[22] This practical advice takes a couple out of the hot seat and places them back in control.

Women often take the brunt of the pressure to have children, but married men also feel the heat. While single, a childless man can go unnoticed (the assumption being that he has simply not been corralled). It is not until he becomes part of a childless couple that he draws attention.

United We Stand

Ironically, what the outside world tries to destroy can sometimes forge a closer bond. Because a couple is forced to bear the brunt of outside criticism together, their marriage often becomes more intimate.

Family, church members, and friends all felt they had the right to probe Peg's decision. "I never felt a vital need to be a mother. It was something I took for granted—a role I could take on if I chose. I made the decision not to have children basically by default. My husband did not want children and when I was twenty-three my ob-gyn told me the chances were good that I could not conceive [due to peritonitis as a child]."

Peg tells about an encounter at her ten-year high school reunion:

A woman I never really liked asked me if I had children. When I said no, she said she was only complete when she became a mother—that it totally fulfilled her. I thought that was a blatant attempt to make me feel like I was not worthy, because I am not a mother. Considering the source, I didn't take it personally, but I remember it, almost fifteen years later. My guess is, she never had an orgasm. I think *that* makes me a woman! At least, it makes me feel more feminine than anything else!

Sometimes the decision not to parent is based on a woman's negative assessment of her mate's parenting abilities. Gretchen is childless at forty-eight. She and her husband did not discuss the subject of children until after they were married. "We didn't think about it. We were young and we were having such a good time. Then after about five or six years, I started thinking about it because my friend was going to have a baby." But Gretchen was not sure about having a child. Each summer, Gretchen's teenaged niece comes to stay for a month. It is a time to which she eagerly looks forward and which gives her an opportunity to explore her mothering needs. And although Gretchen has learned a great deal about herself during these visits, the visits have also revealed something to her about her husband: She is not sure he would be "good father material." He makes attempts with her niece, but she can see that he simply cannot relate to children. Gretchen assessed her husband's discomfort, together with her own reluctance, and decided they were better off childless.

Few couples fine-tune the nitty-gritty decisions of marriage before they wed. Deliberations regarding how money issues will be approached, whose job will take precedence should one partner be offered an out-of-town promotion, and, most important of all, whether children will be in the picture do not occur often enough.

Most of the couples here did discuss children before they wed, thereby eliminating a potential minefield. Others waited until years into the marriage before the subject finally surfaced. What their collective experiences show is that ideally childbearing decisions should be made before one enters marriage.

Unexpectedly Childfree

When Barbie® was first introduced to American girls in 1959, she was an immediate hit.[23] Whatever one may think of her hourglass figure, exotic blue eyes, and luxuriant blonde hair, she nonetheless appealed to youngsters bored with conventional baby dolls. Barbie's tiny feet sported high heels; her almond-shaped eyes boasted bold blue eye shadow; and her apparel (tighter fitting than our mothers deemed proper) was glamorous. Her voluptuous figure spoke volumes about Barbie: This was a sexual creature, a first for dolls. But perhaps most appealing of all to young girls, Barbie lived a jet-setter lifestyle: She did exciting work and had a devoted, muscular boyfriend, Ken.

Barbie had so great an impact on our culture that before long university professors began conducting research to determine her influence on female gender identity. Linda Wason-Ellam, a professor of curriculum studies at the University of Saskatchewan in Canada, concludes, "For young girls, Barbie, especially, appears to be a template of being an ideal girl, a standard against which to judge their own lives."[24] The scholars need not have wasted their time—any six-year-old could have told them the same thing.

There is little doubt that the timing of Barbie's introduction into the marketplace was ideal. The tumultuous 1960s were but a year away and women's restlessness was about to be exposed. As an indication of where we were heading, Barbies, not baby dolls, were what young girls coveted.

Attired in a smart business suit, Barbie entered the culture as a working girl. By 1962, Barbie had acquired a three-story townhouse (obviously having earned enough money for a down payment) and in 1964 started driving a pink hot rod convertible.[25] Before long, the townhouse was upgraded to a spectacular dream house. Barbie was moving up in the world. Just as women's roles have evolved over the forty years since her debut, so has Barbie's. It is hard to know who is mirroring whom.

By the 1980s, Barbie had seemingly penetrated into virtually every profession. No glass ceiling held Barbie down. She went further and faster than any real-life counterpart. Today Barbie is an astronaut, an Olympic gymnast, a horsewoman, a veterinarian, or a dentist, among a myriad of other callings. Barbie is clearly a motivated woman possessing boundless energy.

The only change Barbie has not made in her life is her beau, Ken. Although she has purchased several designer wedding gowns over the past few decades (and even outfitted one or two bridal parties along the way), Barbie has yet to walk down the aisle and make legitimate an obviously committed relationship. Evidently, Barbie does not feel the need for marriage.

And this leads us to a Barbie that will probably never be: Maternity Barbie, complete with an expandable waistline wardrobe. Mattel, inventor of this perennially popular doll, may be on to something in the avoidance of this particular Barbie profile. Young girls appear to be far more interested in exploring a variety of careers available to them (via Barbie) than in merely feeding a boring old baby doll. Girls today are setting their sights on exciting careers and are abandoning not only the baby doll but perhaps real-life babies altogether.

Since 1975, there has been a steady decrease in the number of women having babies. The percentage of U.S. childless women rose from 9 percent in 1975 to 16 percent in 1993. "In the 1970s voluntarily childless women in the U.S. made up about 12.4 percent of the childless population. By 1990, they comprised one-quarter of the childless population."[26] According to the National Center for Health Statistics, "among the entire group of baby-boom women, the figure may climb as high as 20 percent."[27]

The question is: Did Barbie make a conscious decision to forgo motherhood or did time just pass her by? Were her multiple careers so spellbinding that she simply forgot to make plans for having a baby and one day realized it was too late? Or did she discover, as many women do, that life was fulfilling as it was and she didn't feel the need for a child after all?

For the women in this section, childlessness was not so much a conscious choice as it was an evolutionary process. There was no lightning-bolt epiphany, no watershed experience that led them to childlessness. It was simply a place at which they one day arrived. As with Barbie, compelling careers and fruitful relationships sufficed.

Things Change

Sissy comes from a large family. She feels she had the perfect mother. Her mother was a traditionalist. Although wealthy, she made all seven of her children's clothes and cooked gourmet meals for her large brood as well. "She was a great woman," Sissy relates. A former dancer who is now a real estate dynamo, Sissy never planned on childlessness:

I thought I would be the mother of eight children. I was brought up to be a wife and mother! When I married at twenty, we talked about it [having kids], but he was just getting his career going and I didn't want him to change what he was doing or lock him into having to support a child. And I figured I had a lot of time . . . I was selfish enough [that] I wanted to be with [my husband]. All of a sudden, we got comfortable being selfish. I don't believe it was ever a conscious "We're not going to have children." It just happened. I used to feel guilty that something was wrong with me, that I was happy without.

I ask how people regard her childless state. She grins. "With envy. [People say] 'Oh, look what you've missed! You're gonna be alone.' If that's the reason to have children, it's the wrong reason. . . . I hate to think you need a child to fill *anything*."

Some people worry about a future without children. "I have *no* regrets about not having them. I'd worry more if I had them." Sissy admits she drank when she was younger, something she no longer does. "I was a rageaholic [as well], and I was afraid I would take that out on my kids."

Sissy's choice not to have children was partly due to the fact that she did not trust the kind of mother she would be. The decision to not have children is often the most mature one a woman can make. It is a kindness not only to the woman who would not enjoy the role of parent but also to the child who would not be appropriately nurtured.

Janice did her doctoral thesis on childless women. She was drawn to her topic because she herself is childless. She, too, resents the notion that women who cannot or do not have children are seen as diminished.

"My decision evolved. I thought I would have thirteen kids, but then time went by and I didn't have the right partner."

I ask about her adjustment. "At this point [age fifty-four], I'm pretty peaceful. But ten years ago, the recognition was harder." Her voice grows softer. "I knew I was missing out on something quite precious." Contrary to what many people think, most childless women display a perceptive grasp on what they are forgoing when they omit motherhood.

Janice says that despite all the advancements women have made she still observes a negative connotation to childlessness: "It's terrible when childless women are referred to as barren." She grows passionate as she talks: "[That's like] assuming you only have one crop to grow. Fertility may exist in a variety of forms."

Janice, a therapist, is a nurturing woman whose fruitfulness is evident in the lives of her well-cared-for patients. Yet it frustrates her that childless women are somehow viewed as "less than." "Because marriage is central to society, everything else is 'sub.' You're pitied. I just wish this was a nation in which *every* life had value."

The Malicious Moniker

The word "barren" is an anachronistic term for a woman who technically may or may not be able to bear a child. For women who voluntarily choose childlessness, it is not only a misnomer, it is a cruel moniker.

In her book *Barren in the Promised Land*, Elaine Tyler May puts it this way:

> "Barren" is a term laden with historical weight. It carries negative meanings: unproductive, sterile, bare, empty, stark, deficient, lacking, wanting, destitute, devoid. It is the opposite of fertile, lavish, abounding, productive. . . . Yet even today, a powerful stigma surrounds the childless—a stigma that falls more heavily on women. Childlessness is measured in terms of women.[28]

Childless women encounter this nullifying characterization far too frequently. The tenet that a female only becomes a "true woman" when she has given birth nettles many childless women. Female identity, they rightly counter, should not be dependent on merely one of your choices in life.

Mardy Ireland wrote in her book *Reconceiving Women: Separating Motherhood from Female Identity*, "No woman, mother or not, will ever be free to fully explore her capacities as a human being if the only valid role in which to feel she is an adult or a 'real woman' is that of a mother. A woman should not have to be left feeling that she has a hole in her identity, is unnatural, or is threatening to others simply because she is not a mother."[29]

"It Just Turned Out This Way"

Ramey is a childless woman who concurs with Ireland's assessment. She grew up believing she would one day be married with children. She married and has a career as a television producer, but she did not have children:

> There was no conscious decision about not having kids. I never sat down and said no, I'm not going to have a child. I just feel this is the path life took. I'm the classic person who slid into it. . . . Oops! I forgot to have kids.
>
> I married [for the first time] at forty-three. As soon as I started trying [to get pregnant], it was already too late for fertility treatments. Now doctors are more liberal. [But] when I went, they were using donor eggs.
>
> I got to the point when I didn't want to put my body through that. So I slid into it. If I had gotten pregnant right after we'd gotten married, that would have been great. And we tried. We even considered adopting.

She pauses and looks out the restaurant window. "At this point, at forty-eight, I think, frankly, do I really have the energy to do this? It's all I can do to think about what I'm going to do about retirement. Right now would be a better time, but I don't know that I have the energy for it."

For Ramey, one of the most painful aspects has been the occasional dismissal by people in social situations.

"People feel comfortable questioning you, 'Why don't you have kids?' 'Are you going to adopt?' 'Do you *want* to have kids?' This is very pointed." I ask if it was any different when she was single. She sits back and considers. "People are much more willing to accept women who aren't married as opposed to a woman who is married, has a home and a good relationship, and doesn't have a child. 'What's wrong with *you*?'"

She shakes her head. "Like at an Easter egg hunt [at a friend's house]. I was there helping prepare at 7 A.M. Someone later said to me, 'Which one is yours?' I said, 'I don't have any,' and she moved on."

Ramey's tone is incredulous. "They'll go on to someone they can talk to about the kids, the little league, the school. I'm *completely* dismissed. Usually, it's not that blatant, but it has been. I can be dismissed because I don't have kids."

Dr. Jan Cameron, a sociologist, validates Ramey's experience in a study she conducted focusing on what it is like to be a nonparent in a world that expects parenting to be an assumed adult role. She sees the move toward intentional childlessness as a "demographic phenomenon heralding a shift in fertility values" and writes:

People who choose not to have children are often cloaked in mystery, described in stereotypes. They are expected to explain *why* they do not have children—parents are very rarely expected to explain why they *do* have children. Stereotypically, non-parents are seen as selfish, neurotic, immature or abnormal. They flout conventional wisdom. They have actively chosen not to do what most people take for granted as normal.[30]

Abigail, a fifty-year-old woman who grew up in the Midwest, would hardly be considered abnormal or a woman who flouts convention. A petite lady with a gentle grace, she evokes the image of Audrey Hepburn. One feels peaceful in her presence. It is no wonder that her counseling practice is thriving. Abigail sits demurely in her overstuffed office chair and tells me about her life.

Abigail's first marriage ended in divorce, and at age thirty-five she became engaged to her present husband. "I always thought we would have kids. We talked about it in a very general, vague way and then in my late thirties I decided to go back to school. And to my surprise, and really to my amazement, I really loved school." Abigail chuckles. Then her mood becomes more thoughtful.

"The summer of my fortieth birthday I thought, well, if I'm ever going to have kids, I really need to do something about it. And I need to do something about it *now*." She combs her hair with slender fingers.

I had a number of friends who had kids in their forties and I didn't look upon them with envy. They were exhausted and I didn't necessarily want to do that. Then I felt, would I really be able to pull off starting a new career if I go through a pregnancy and have a baby? What kind of a career am I going to have? What? I'm going to be a part-time mom, a part-time working woman?

She sighs and sits back in her chair. "It just didn't seem like having kids in my forties made any sense. So all summer, I found myself looking at infants, and it was interesting. By the end of the summer, I thought, I'm not going to make myself crazy. I'm going to make a decision one way or another. So I made a choice."

I ask her if she has any regrets. She reflects for a moment. When she speaks, it is deliberately. "I regret not having had a family with my husband. But I don't regret it in any kind of way that eats away at me."

Does she feel a woman's identity is defined by mothering? Her voice becomes firm:

> I don't think that motherhood has anything to do with being a woman. I think one of the things the feminists have done is educate a lot of men, and also a lot of women, that one can be a live, functioning woman and not be a mother. One of the things they [people] talk about is that women who don't have children are selfish and that always takes me aback when I hear that. You know, I think so many people have kids because *they're* selfish and *they* want to have a clone and it's very much about them.

Her gentle demeanor is gone. "Talk about selfish . . . I don't get women who have babies and leave them with a caregiver." She has finished her diatribe and settles back. But she is not done. "So I think, as a matter of fact, that just the opposite is true. I think people who chose not to have children are not selfish, and the people I know who don't have kids have given children a great deal of thought. A *great* deal of thought. I don't know anyone who does not have a child who hasn't agonized over the decision."

The Checklist

Marilyn, herself childless, is a godmother many times over. Although fond of children, she never wanted any herself. Marilyn reveals an ugly side to parenting that she has witnessed:

> There are some women I know who've had children who are not particularly nurturing. I once had a woman say to me, a tremendously successful woman, that "I got married a few years ago, I've just had a kid and now I can spend all my time on my career because I've gotten those things done with." It was absolutely horrifying to me. It was like a checklist. I'm checking this off, I'm checking that off.

The irony, Marilyn feels, is that the woman with the child feels herself morally superior to Marilyn.

What Is Normal?

The struggle to properly define childless women remains ellusive. It is an uphill battle to reformulate years of revocatory thinking, especially when it is a part of the therapeutic world—the world where "normalcy" is supposedly defined. Mardy Ireland, in her book *Reconceiving Woman*, states:

> Classical psychoanalytic theory regarding female development has justified and supported a portrayal of women who aren't mothers as deficient or negative, viewing them as unable or unwilling to fulfill a feminine role. Since psychoanalysis is the most significant psychological perspective in this century, shaping our understanding of the human psyche, the impact of this negative and incomplete portrayal of female identity has been substantial. Male reproductive functioning and fatherhood are not the centerpieces for adult male developmental theory, but female reproductive capacity has become central and definitive for normative female development. . . . There is an implicit assumption that motherhood is intrinsic to adult female identity. This assumption necessarily implies an "absence" for any woman who is not a mother.[31]

Fighting a presumption this lethal is daunting. Equality cannot be circumscribed to include only certain segments of the female population. If women are honest in their bid for equality, then it must be across the board, and childless women must be embraced.

Since the late 1960s, various segments of the American population have come forth to claim their rightful place at the table: minorities, disabled persons, gays, the chemically dependent, the medically challenged (e.g., those with dyslexia, attention deficit disorder, Tourette's syndrome), the sexually or emotionally abused, and the mentally ill. For each group, educating the public as to who they are was essential for gaining acceptance. One group glaringly missing from the above list is childless women. Elizabeth Dole, Oprah Winfrey, Janet Reno, and Gloria Steinem have all helped expand our appreciation for the talents of childless women, but it is the everyday childless woman who needs respectability.

The women in this section make clear that their decision to remain childless was a very personal, very clear choice. Although it may have been reached by a circuitous route, it is nonetheless one they have never regretted.

MISCONCEPTIONS

It does me good to be alone.

—Louisa May Alcott[1]

4

Misconceptions

I must confess that when I began writing this book, I believed that deep down every woman wanted to mother. Since it was *my* dream, I audaciously assumed it was a dream shared by others. I was compelled to write this book because something in me wanted to know the truth—although what that truth was, I was not sure. Perhaps I wanted to know I could have survived if my fondest wish—motherhood—had been denied me. I now believe there was something much greater I was meant to discover. In the beginning, however, I thought every woman wanted children. I had a lot to learn.

Interview by interview, woman by woman, story by story, my beliefs were challenged. Aside from those who could not achieve a much desired pregnancy, I met happy, contented women who just happened to be childless. Even those I spoke with who were tragically childless had even-

tually found peace. These women were vibrant and fulfilled. Walking into their worlds, I found genuine serenity.
Their lives were self-directed, not selfish, as I was led to
believe. Before long, I was no longer asking, "How would I
have been without a child?" I wanted to know, "Who
would I be if I were free to choose the way I spend my energies?" I began seeing the benefits of a childless life,
something I had not known would exist.

I liked the women I met. They were complex and exceedingly honest. They displayed self-deprecating humor.
There were only two women with whom I had difficulty
empathizing. I felt their childlessness stemmed from issues
that remained unresolved and unexamined. The other
women (well over 100) had spent numerous hours contemplating their childlessness. Although some certainly wished
to mother, the majority said they emphatically did not—
never had—and I believed them. Finally.

In the middle of writing this book, one of my daughter's
school friends was killed in an accident. The family was
devastated and friends worried about the length and
depth of the mother's grief. To be near Liza, to witness
her pain and be helpless to ease it, was torturous. There
was no relief, only endurance for her, through those first
months. For her friends, there was guilt that our children
survived when hers did not, and there developed a more
concrete fear that lightning could strike twice and that
sharing her grief did not protect us from ever experiencing it. It was with this awareness that I was laboring to
write this book.

Occasionally, I grew jealous of the childless women with whom I was speaking. They were free and I was not. They would never be subject to the kind of pain Liza was living with and that I was vulnerable to. I saw childlessness in a new light, a light I would never bask in. The old saw, "'tis better to have loved and lost,"[2] felt too cruel a consequence for making the decision to parent. I questioned how wise it was to mother.

I learned a valuable lesson through this event: the importance of never pushing your desire on another. What if I had talked a woman into mothering—because it had been right for me—and she suffered Liza's loss? The drive to bolster every woman's choice became more vital.

I began this journey as a skeptic. I am now a believer. We are all different beings with different needs. This was something I thought I knew, but did not. The women I interviewed taught me this truth. It was a rite of passage that has altered me forever.

Reality Check

There were many distinct discoveries I made in my exploration into childlessness. Probably foremost is the clear recognition that childlessness is the very large elephant in our collective living room. It grows bigger and more formidable every day, but no one wants to admit it is here. Although 42.2 percent of the adult female population is childless,[3] these women—and the option—are still treated as though they do not exist. Childless women permeate our world. They are our neighbors, our coworkers, our sisters, and our best friends. But because these women do not conform to traditional roles, their existence is denied. Sociologists confirm this: "Increasing expanses of childlessness in women's lives and selective neglect of childlessness as a research topic means that there is a discrepancy between what is going on in women's lives and the concepts and ideas employed to understand these."[4]

The sheer lack of coverage this topic receives in the media speaks volumes. Advertisers, politicians, and educators fail to target childless women as a group. Again, these women are seemingly nonexistent. What little knowledge we do have of childless women is based on negative stereotypes, such as the child-hating workaholic. Our personal knowledge of these women may tell us otherwise, but the accepted viewpoint remains cynical.

"Tell Me Something Positive"

We maintain this negative view of childlessness, I believe, because we know nothing about the positive side. It has never been extolled. It is considered "unwomanly" to admit to feeling happy and whole without children. Yet the childless women I talked to shared with me a myriad of benefits: the latitude to develop their careers fully; the intimacy they share with their mates; the lack of financial, emotional, and time pressures; the freedom from fear of being a bad mother or having a difficult child; the spiritual growth that takes place thanks to the availability of unfettered time; the relief of not having to raise a loved one in a world some view as too violent or too selfish. These were just some of the advantages they enjoyed. How ironic that we support the notion that retired people should travel and enjoy themselves, yet we reject the idea of a younger couple doing so.

"You Will Regret It"

One remark that seemed particularly cruel to me was the warning these women received about a dire future. Not only are childless women told they are selfish for not having children (many interviewees reported being told this), but perfect strangers feel completely comfortable warning these women about a lonely old age. It takes gargantuan strength to defend against this kind of pessimism, particularly since few of us are ever 100 percent certain about any decision we make in life. I was happy to pass along some good news to the women I interviewed. *The reality of a lonely old age is negated by every study ever done:* "[There is] no significant differences in loneliness and depression between parents and childless adults."[5] Yet childless women remain uninformed in this regard. The news is not spectacular, nor controversial enough to find its way into *Vanity Fair,* the *New York Times,* or *Harper's Bazaar.* So these women live their lives having to filter negative information on a regular basis, praying the warnings do not come to pass. Each woman I told was visibly relieved to hear the results of these studies.

Where Are the Educators?

Education, which should be key to correcting the misconceptions about childless women, is failing us as a society. I could find no college or university with a women's study course that explored the topic of childlessness, although many discuss motherhood. It is as though female childlessness does not exist (the elephant in the living room again). One professor of sociology who lectures on women's studies proudly told me of the two pieces she uses that allude to childlessness. One is a documentary about a child looking for the mother who abandoned her when she was an infant, and the other is a book about a woman who gave up her child because she did not feel she was capable of being a good mother. Not only were these examples *not* about childless women, they presented negative assessments of women after they already had children. Most of the women I met made positive choices, not after-the-fact ones. When I pointed this out, the professor bristled. She could not see the difference.

In Denial

A group of women that affected me deeply were those who had been unable to come to terms with not having children. It is hard, particularly for single women, to acknowledge that they may never have children, so they engage in what I call mental mothering. These are women, often forty-five or older, who still believe pregnancy is a possibility. Because these women are ovulating, they believe they are adequately fertile and that childbearing is an option for them. In reality, it would not only be difficult, it would be improbable. Saying "I will never have a child" is difficult for some women to accept, so they never actually make the decision.

Morgan, forty-five, exemplifies many to whom I spoke. She talks of repeatedly pushing the decision to mother into the background, especially when she is engaged in a project at work, only to have it resurface later. She then renegotiates with herself the date for making the final call. In the times between self-negotiations, one or another medical discovery surfaces, giving her renewed reason to delay her decision. This allows her to postpone the decision even longer. During moments of clarity, however, Morgan realizes she more than likely will never mother and sinks into a deep depression.

The cultural mantras to which women adhere—take charge, go for it, be in control—need some retooling when one lives in the real world. Few people get it all, and some do not want it all, but for the Morgans of the world, it is hard to let go of a dream she did want. "I feel like a failure as a woman," she admitted. "I'm a woman and it's my function to reproduce. If I don't, then why am I here?" To complicate matters, Morgan's unhappiness with being childless is exacerbated by self-reproachment. She was married at a young age but did not want a baby at the time. Much to her surprise, she found herself divorced at age thirty-three. As she matured, Morgan found her mothering needs, but she never found another mate.

Until childless women are accepted as complete human beings just as they are, women like Morgan will continue to berate themselves for something over which they had little or no control.

Mothers, Teach Your Daughters Well

Although older women like Morgan are aware that time is running short, of major concern to me as I spoke to younger women was their lack of information about childbearing and childlessness. Other than some sketchy knowledge about the pill, these women knew little about conception, other than how it takes place. It seems that no one (not even their mothers or their gynecologists) is talking to young women about the facts regarding conception. Until I lectured college-aged women about pregnancy statistics and miscarriage rates at different stages in a woman's life, they were unaware that choosing when to have a baby is critical.[6] It strikes me as absolutely necessary that we provide these young women with clearer information about reproduction. Most of the tragically childless told me the first time they were made aware of these statistics was when they consulted a fertility specialist—when they were already in trouble. Women have made significant advances and may indeed be more empowered in the workplace these days, but they are crippled by ignorance when it comes to this aspect of their personal lives.

The problem seems easily rectifiable. Gynecologists should provide on a regular basis updated statistical information to their patients that informs women of their reproductive capabilities at each stage in life. This should come with any birth control information a women receives. No woman should be childless due to poor timing or lack of knowledge.

Certainly, the media is partially responsible. The story of a sixty-two-year-old Italian woman having a baby makes good copy. Headlines that scream "A Big Boost in Multiple Births"[7] and "Menopausal Woman Gets Ovary Transplant"[8] give distorted information and create false hope in women who are predicating major life decisions on innuendo and hype. If women are to be in charge of their lives, they must be informed. Remaining ignorant of the facts does not prevent a woman from falling victim to them.

Doctors and mothers should provide their patients and daughters with a *complete* list of their options: how to prevent a pregnancy, statistical chances of achieving a pregnancy at each stage in life, how to obtain an abortion, how to obtain RU-486 and ECP pills, how adoptions work, *plus* the benefits of childlessness. This would truly empower young women and allow them to make informed decisions about what is best for their lives.

Motherhood as a Choice

Just as childlessness is a complex subject, so is mothering. Parenting for me has been the most expansive, enhancing event of my life. It has made me a happier, more fulfilled human being. I make better choices than I would have done if my daughter had not been in my world. Yet who spoke of the great spiritual experience I would know by having my child? Or the tremendous bond it would create with my husband? Women cannot make informed decisions unless they have all the information, including the positives as well as the negatives of both choices.

Childless women and mothers should be encouraged, not circumscribed, to talk about their experiences so that younger women have a greater understanding about the choices available to them.

The She Generation

One discovery that surprised me while researching and writing this book was the generational gap with regard to women's feelings about their childlessness. Women in their fifties acknowledged a strong societal imperative toward having children, which in turn (as with Morgan) left them feeling inadequate because they had not. Women in their forties had mixed reactions. Some felt there was a societal expectation placed on them, whereas others did not. Women under thirty-five did not feel this sense of obligation. The society these women grew up in is one more open to allowing individuals to make their own choice, thereby allowing younger, more liberated women to be comfortable with childlessness. The next generation could well be childless with impunity.

Dealing with It

Childless women were eager to talk not only about themselves but about the world they inhabit. They were filled with frustrations, which as I heard them tumble out, I understood.

A major frustration for these women is people who do not believe that they truly did not want a child. People think they are kidding, can be coaxed into childbearing, or have something emotionally wrong with them. Even I was guilty of these assumptions when I began this book. Society still clings to the definition of woman = mother. "Biological *possibility* and desire are not the same as biological *need*," the author Betty Rollins observes. "Women have child-bearing equipment. For them to choose not to use the equipment is no more blocking what is instinctive than it is for a man who, muscles or no, chooses not to be a weightlifter."[9] The way we separate femininity from fertility is by acknowledging that childbearing is an option, not an obligation. Women are spiritually whole with or without children. It is natural to have or not have children.

Another assumption that drives some childless women to distraction is that they will deposit their mothering needs into some other source: their animals or a career such as nursing or teaching. Although some women do this, others recoil at the notion: "I am tired of being lumped into the nurturer, domestic, craft-loving stereotype just because of my sex. Why do we have to be nurturers of the world just because we're women? What's wrong with just being ourselves?" Lynda asked. Just as all mothers are not alike, neither are all childless women. It is not simply that these particular childless women do not want children; they do not want to nourish, cherish, or indulge *anything*. We find it amusing or endearing when a man goes against stereotype and does something like needlepoint, but we are suspicious of a woman who does not wish to nurture. I truly believe we limit what it means to be a woman if we define womanhood within the narrow confines of motherhood alone.

Respecting our differences is essential. One woman clarified her feelings this way:

> It is often difficult to understand the choices other people make. I can no more understand how my best friend feels about giving birth to her daughter than I can imagine winning a marathon, performing cardiac surgery, playing a violin concerto, or walking the ocher streets of Kathmandu with a begging bowl. We give birth to ideas, to relationships, to works of art, to hope, to peace, to children, and to each other.

Fair Is Fair

Of major concern to me is discovering that childless women and mothers are in two adversarial camps. We view each other with suspicion rather than with acceptance. The clash that once raged between working mothers and stay-at-home mothers seems to have taken a backseat to the new debate between working mothers and childless workers. Childless women I spoke with expressed growing frustration with the superior stance some mothers take.

An example of our adversarial positions is clear in the following episodes: Susan told about a conversation she had with a friend who has four children. The mother had to make a last-minute out-of-town trip and said to her, "You don't know what I have to go through to go away!" Susan felt slighted that her life and her responsibilities were not regarded as being as important as her friend's. I saw both sides of this conversation. Leaving four children would require major juggling, especially if it was a last-minute trip. Children have play dates, doctor's appointments, school, sports . . . the list goes on. The friend who had to go out of town may not have meant to be dismissive, but in fact she was. Is her life more important than her friend's? Certainly not; it is just more encumbered. Is the childless woman overly sensitive? Perhaps.

Another childless woman told me it was a terrible message a mother was sending her son when she bought him a truck "so he wouldn't get killed on the road. She's telling her son that his life is the only one that counts." When I suggested that I thought it instinctive to protect those you love, she vehemently disagreed. She insisted it was a mother creating a selfish child. Mothers, it would appear, do not have an exclusive on being judgmental.

Kate was upset when her friend's son had a play-off game on what turned out to be Kate's birthday. She understood, but was irritated she had to make other plans for dinner.

Birthdays only come once a year, yet a mother's first obligation is to her child. Each woman was torn.

Judith, who has no children, told me about going to her sister's house at Christmastime. Although she loves being with everyone, no one ever asks after her or her husband. The entire schedule is planned around the children. The "family" is what counts, and she is peripheral family at best. But she says nothing because (a) she does not want to ruin the holiday, and (b) she is afraid she would be viewed as selfish if she spoke up.

Ideally, women should communicate their feelings when these moments occur. Childless women and mothers cannot know what each other's world is truly like. You cannot baby-sit and think you comprehend the responsibilities of parenting. Conversely, parents cannot assume their past knowledge of the single life is in any way applicable to that which their friends live.

Codependent

The environmentally childless kept reminding me that it is irresponsible to procreate without thought to the consequence; that a world overrun with children would cause extinction. Yet I could not help but think that, conversely, a world without children could not function. Baby boomers will need Gen-X doctors as they age and, in kind, the Gen-Xers will want the succeeding generation to care for them. Individuals who produce children provide the world with needed resources. Childless women may supply the equilibrium nature needs to maintain a healthy balance. In other words, we need each other. It is time we acknowledge and embrace one another for the gifts that each of us brings to this planet. For either side to point to the other as inferior and themselves as superior is destructive and dishonest.

Where We Are Headed

To be sure, as the number of childless women grows, a new political force will be felt. The inequalities the childless have endured will be less tolerated and demands will be made for corrections. The childless women I spoke to were articulate and fair-minded in their assessments of where those changes must be made.

At Work

The first place that requires change is the workplace. It is there that the childless face a daily barrage of unfair practices. In *The Baby Boon: How Family-Friendly America Cheats the Childless*,[10] Elinor Burkett addresses the topic head on: The childless worker is abused. The conflict in the workplace, she claims, is no longer men versus women; it is the childless worker versus the parent worker. At first, I suspected the women I spoke with might be exaggerating, but the more stories they related to me, the better I understood.

When I read that Betty Friedan (a grandmother) hung up on Burkett when she called to interview her for her book, I was shocked. When Burkett told her the nature of the book,

Friedan screamed at Burkett, "Why are you doing this?"[11] The blatant unfairness the childless worker endured did not register (or matter) to Friedan. I was stunned by this exchange. Here was the woman who led the way! Here was the woman who stated that *all* women need to work together, and yet here she was rejecting important information *about* women. Friedan has a vested interest in working mothers because she feels they have a difficult time in corporate America, but if Friedan cannot sense the importance of inclusion, who can? Why are the needs of the working mother and the childless worker seen as mutually exclusive? Friedan's claim that this type of discussion pits women against women ignores the cry of those who are being treated unfairly. Since when do we champion only half a group? Until all women are respected for whatever choices they make, *we are not liberated*. It is our obligation to protect—and include—one another, at home and in the workplace.

Childless employees clarified for me how they are often shortchanged when it comes to medical benefits. Although many companies have addressed the issue by offering cafeteria plans, giving employees a set amount of money to spend on a choice of benefits, many employees say those plans solve only part of the problem. Anita, an Oregon woman, gave a concrete example. The company where she works formerly provided 100 percent coverage for employees and partial coverage for their dependents. To provide better coverage for dependents, overall coverage for employees was reduced. The childless were in essence asked to subsidize the families of other employees with a cut to their own benefits. "We had some meetings. At first no one spoke up. You're made to feel as though you're selfish. I was losing something for the benefit of people with kids." Before long, one disgruntled childless employee voiced discontent to another, then another, and another. Eventually, they presented their case to their boss, who was surprised at all the fuss. "There were a lot of hurt feelings." But the childless employees did not prevail. Round one went to the working parents.

Some childless women told me they are tired of working longer hours, traveling more, or otherwise picking up the slack for colleagues with family obligations. Victoria, who lives in California's Hollywood Hills, is childless and works with a few parent-employees. She understands when a male coworker leaves early to tend to his parenting chores. Everyone in the company knows that Bill (not his real name) carries his beeper with him so he can be reached when necessary. But it is Bill who is always excused early from meetings and it is Bill who has to be tracked down when someone cannot find an important document in his office. Sometimes Bill can be found; other times his beeper is not answered. In short, Victoria respects his right to parent, but she feels it is a pain in the neck when it comes to conducting work. Conversely, Victoria is equally concerned about a female coworker. She recalls an instance when the woman's child was ill and running a fever. Rather than miss a meeting, the woman arranged for the sitter to stay longer with her child, something that made Victoria uncomfortable. Shouldn't a mother be home with her sick child? she wondered. The same questions that plague parents plague sensitive childless workers. They worry that the need in the workplace to get a job done can contribute to some children being neglected. This creates an emotional burden on many childless employees. Appropriate boundaries have not been established for the working parent and the childless employee so that each feels clear about what is expected in the workplace.

Yet because of the stamp of approval motherhood receives, it has been impossible to say what is on most childless workers' minds, namely, why do I have to pick up the slack at work for a decision *you* made? Whose idea was it to have kids, anyway?

Many childless workers are tired of being overworked, uncompensated for the extra work, and viewed as second-class citizens despite extra efforts. In an era when equal pay for equal work is the standard, equal respect for choice is sadly not in place. Regrettably, the needs of the working mother are considered noble whereas the needs of the childless are viewed as unimportant or even frivolous. Nonetheless, one woman's goals should not be achieved at the cost of the rights of another.

Burkett sums up the dilemma with a question: "Mothers expect childless people to cover as if it's an entitlement. The fact that it inconveniences me never registers. I've yet to meet any parent who felt at all guilty about ripping off a childless person. The women's movement gave women choices. . . . But why am I expected to do more because someone else chose to do too much?"[12]

The Upside

At the same time, it must also be admitted that the news for the childless employee is not all negative. Despite these subtle discriminations, childless women have seen advantages to being childless. In fact, when applying for a new job these days, many tout their state: I'm not married so there's no one to consult if I want to work late. Also, I have no husband who could be transferred out of town if he gets promoted. Add to that, no child who can get sick, no child who plays basketball or needs to go to the dentist. You bet I announce my childlessness. What employer wouldn't want me? they ask.

In *Flying Solo: Single Women in Midlife*, Carol Anderson and Susan Stewart examined the lives of working single and childless women:

> Being single can be a serious advantage for women in the workplace. While single women are not on equal footing with their male counterparts in most organizations, they often have an edge over women who are married. Employers tend to view single women as having fewer demands competing for their time and energies, particularly if they do not have dependent children. . . . Single women are seen as "fair game" for extra projects that require staying late or working weekends to meet deadlines. Employers assume that they should be dependable and available, and they often are.
>
> Many single women who make themselves available in times of crises and deadlines move into positions of steadily increasing responsibility as their special qualities become evident.[13]

As a supervisor who hires employees, Devon says that a prospective employee's childlessness is a definite consideration. For the childless employee who wants to get ahead, being willing to pick up the slack for parent-employees can sometimes be advantageous: "Angela worked her way from a minimum-wage menial job to vice-president by always offering to help whichever colleague was in the next job up the ladder, thereby learning the tasks of that job."[14]

It may well be that the childless worker will have the fastest climb up the corporate ladder. Finally, after years of being treated as "less than," childless workers are demanding changes and putting a new twist on the notion of who is the reliable employee.

Taxing Issues

Undoubtedly, taxes will be another area that will begin to be addressed as the number of women remaining childless grows and they become more vocal. Politicians may have ignored the childless voter in past elections, but I doubt they can do so for much longer. The childless women I spoke with do not balk at contributing to schools they will never utilize, but tax credits for families with children is another matter entirely to them. "This is going to sound bitter," a childless worker named Dana tells me, "but I think our tax system is unfairly slanted toward families and nonworking women." Many childless women are fearful of speaking their minds for the same reason Dana mentioned—they don't want to sound bitter. So they remain silent and accept the clear favoritism awarded parents. Figures, however, do not lie. In 1999, a childless couple with a combined earned salary of $70,000 paid $10,455 in taxes. A couple with two children paid $7,915, a difference of $2,540. One tax agent told me, "Social economics dictates everything the government is going to allow you to take as a credit on your income taxes. What the government likes you to do, you get a credit for—such as buying a house or having children; what they don't want you to do—such as gambling—they don't allow."[15] Certainly, children cost far more than this tax break, but these kinds of examples speak to why childless workers feel mistreated.

Be It Ever So Humble

There is no place like home. That is, unless your castle is feeling invaded. Consider the woman who actively dislikes children and whose apartment abuts one inhabited by a teenager enamored with heavy-metal music. Worse off is the woman who spent years trying to get pregnant, only to be left emotionally bereft and without a child. She is forced to hear the squeals of someone else's toddler in the hallways of her apartment complex or racing down the sidewalk. Although this woman may emotionally need to be away from children, at least for the time being, she cannot be. The U.S. Fair Housing Act of 1998 prevents discrimination based on race, nationality, sex, or disabilities. Also included is familial status. In the United States, unless a building is designated for seniors, a parent or any person with legal custody of a child under eighteen years of age may not be denied housing.[16] This nationwide law means childless women younger than fifty-five years of age are restricted to living side by side with children—whether they wish to or not. This is reverse discrimination and demands redress.

Childless Women of Achievement

Pride in one's identity is important. In recent decades, various groups have developed their own traditions to acknowledge and applaud those successful individuals with whom they share important characteristics. Childless women have never been applauded (let alone acknowledged) as a group. Most people are unaware that many important women, past and present, are or were childless. Their personal achievements are so enormous that often they overshadow their private stories. Taking a look at who some of these childless women are reminds us of just how inappropriate the term "barren" is for any of them.

Oprah Winfrey, producer, actress, and talk show host, is forthright in her position: "I don't have any regrets about not having babies. . . . You can't have it all at one time."[17] Like the Academy Award–winning actress Katharine Hepburn before her, Winfrey is positively childfree. She is well known for her philanthropic and political efforts aimed at improving the lives of children. Another famous childless woman is Gloria Steinem, an author and a leader in the women's liberation movement. She has long been outspoken about the fact that she has not wanted children. Although she reversed her stance against marriage in 2000 by marrying at age sixty-six,[18] it is clearly too late to change her mind about having children. The feminist author Germaine Greer has also actively chosen not to have children.

We cannot presume to know the true cause of childlessness in women who lived in earlier times. Biographers rarely explore the issue, undoubtedly because discussing a woman's childlessness was even more taboo in years gone by. But certainly, the actions of some women of achievement indicate that children were a low (if not nonexistent priority) in their lives.

Women devoted to their careers often make a conscious decision to remain childless. Florence Nightingale turned down a marriage proposal from a man she loved because she feared a home life would interfere with her goals.[19] A number of childless women of note could well have been childless by choice: silent screen legend and studio founder Mary Pickford (who also cofounded the city of Beverly Hills), actress-dancer Ginger Rogers, prima ballerina Margot Fonteyn, psychoanalyst Anna Freud, opera diva Maria Callas, choreographer Agnes de Mille, fashion designer Coco Chanel, daredevil reporter Nelly Bly, and aviator Amelia Earhart were wholly dedicated to their work. Famed artist Mary Cassatt was fond of children but completely committed to her art. Aware that a conventional life would not be possible if she was to paint, Cassatt once remarked, "An artist must be capable of making the primary sacrifices."[20] Cassatt's sensitive mother/child portraits are considered some of the finest in the world.

Think of the literature of writers Dorothy Parker, Ayn Rand, Lillian Hellman, Beatrix Potter, Isak Dinesen, Rachel Carson, Margaret Mitchell, Jane Austen, Helen Keller, Emily Brontë, and Simone de Beauvoir. Or the talents of choreographer Martha Graham, photo-journalist Margaret Bourke-White, costume designer Edith Head, artist Georgia O'Keeffe, and the famed athlete Babe Didrikson Zaharias, to name but a few. These women have enriched our lives immensely in ways other than bringing children into the world.

Mother Theresa, like all Catholic nuns, was religiously childless. Her commitment to her religious order precluded her having children, but her devotion to them was evident.

Environmental issues, although always a concern, are relatively new in the general consciousness. The environmentally childfree, however, possess the same political passion of yesteryear's suffragettes. Susan B. Anthony cofounded the National Woman Suffrage Association. Lydia Marie Child, best known for her poem "Over the River and Through the Woods," was also a passionate champion of equal rights.

One cannot help but admire and be baffled by the sheer physical ability of these women to remain childless. They did so at a time when birth control was notoriously unreliable and abortions were not only dangerous but illegal.

Anaïs Nin had several abortions—a risky practice in the days before its legalization.[21]

Many important women faced medical and emotional challenges to becoming mothers. Frida Kahlo, Mexico's best-known female artist, was six when she was diagnosed with polio. When she was fifteen, Kahlo's life was transformed by a freakish accident. The trolley car in which she was riding was struck by a car and a handrail tore into her abdomen. She endured thirty surgeries after the accident and was in constant pain. Kahlo was married to the famed artist Diego Rivera and was desperate for children, some feminist historians say even obsessive.[22] Unfortunately, she suffered three miscarriages. Art critics often remark that her emotional pain is evident in her haunting self-portraits.

Virginia Woolf suffered her first mental breakdown at the age of thirteen. When she was thirty, she married Leonard Woolf and did find some measure of happiness. Due to her recurring bouts of manic depression, however, Leonard felt it would be better for Virginia to remain childless. Although she often expressed a desire to have children, eventually she gave up. Her biographer James King writes, "She was sadly aware she had killed the desire to have children instinctively; as perhaps nature does."[23] Woolf never managed to overcome her battle with mental illness, despite her great success as a writer and the devotion of her husband.

Poet Emily Dickinson was said to be fond of children. She was known to lower baskets of gingerbread from her window to the children below.[24] During her lifetime, only seven of Emily Dickinson's poems were published. Virginia Woolf and Emily Dickinson were victims of severe bouts of depression. Today, these women's illnesses would be treated, and presumably controlled, with the use of antidepressants. Despite their challenges, these women created masterful works of art while battling personal demons and painful childlessness.

Clara Barton founded the American Red Cross after tirelessly ministering to soldiers during the Civil War. She was courted by many men yet turned down all proposals. Biographers postulate that her parents' contentious marriage was probably the reason she never wed.[25]

Annie Oakley of Wild West fame grew up in an abusive household. During her lifetime, she taught over 15,000 women how to use a gun. It is certainly possible that Oakley's chosen profession and her childlessness were linked to her childhood.

Jane Addams's mother died when Addams was two years of age. When she was seventeen, her father died and she became gravely ill. Years later, she opened Hull House, thereby establishing the field of social work in the United States. In 1931, she became the first woman to receive the Nobel Peace Prize.[26] Perhaps Addams's painful childhood contributed to her decision to devote herself to her work rather than risk more personal loss.

The author Louisa May Alcott grew up in impoverished circumstances. When *Little Women* was introduced, Alcott was thirty-six years of age. The book was an immediate success and Alcott became the sole breadwinner of the family. These familial pressures could easily cause a woman to shun the idea of beginning a new family and adding more responsibilities to her life.

Undoubtedly, some women who never married adhered to societal dictates and remained virgins, thereby eliminating any possibility for mothering. Other than Elizabeth I of England, few celebrated women declared their virginity; thus we may never know who else may be childless by standards. Speculation abounds as to why Elizabeth I chose to be the Virgin Queen, but she is revered, even today, as an exemplary monarch.

Childless women stand in good company. There is reason for them to be proud.

What the Experts Say

When I began studying childless women, I was sure I would find mountains of material and research on the topic. There was very little. I could find only two professors who had done doctoral theses that related to the topic of childlessness. I asked a multitude of universities, institutes, and polling groups if they had statistics on childless women. Most replied, "No, but that's a great subject." Of the twenty-five major universities I contacted, only one could address the issue. These are schools with departments in women's studies, human development, social research, demography, science research, sociology, family studies, and population studies. Those I did speak with reiterated what I had heard before: "We haven't done any research in that area. We probably should." Other than the U.S. Census Bureau, no agency is specifically tracking childless women.

It would be helpful to know how the increase in childlessness will affect women in the future. Luckily, there are some groups that have studied family trends. This research inadvertently related to childlessness because of the nature of the changes that have occurred in family structure over the past fifty years.

I spoke with David Blankenhorn from the Institute for American Values. Blankenhorn expressed genuine concern about the expansion of childlessness in our culture. The fact that we are not reproducing ourselves at an adequate replacement rate was worrisome to him. "We're marching out of history," he told me. "We're pulling our own plug. In a deep sense, when a culture decides it doesn't want to continue, that suggests something very problematic. [It indicates that] we've lost confidence in our own civilization. It's troubling." When I mentioned that the immigrant population seems to be balancing our population needs he noted, "Now we're depending on immigrants not only to *care* for our children, but also to *supply* them."[27]

I spoke to Tom Smith, director of the Social Survey at the University of Chicago. He, too, sees a big shift in the American family and a decline in the ideal number of children. I asked him about Blankenhorn's assessment. Smith's concern is that we cannot rely on immigrants to supply the country with children. "Immigrant populations will eventually decrease their family sizes," he said. "There isn't one immigrant group—the Poles, the Italians, the Jews—that didn't go through that [decreased family sizes] as they moved up the scale. We have no reason to believe that that will not happen with the East Asian and Latin groups as well."

U.N. projections seem to support both men's claims. According to the United Nations, fertility rates in the following countries are currently below replacement level: the United States, Ireland, Norway, China, Australia, Denmark, the United Kingdom, France, Sweden, Belgium, Canada, Switzerland, Japan, Germany, Italy, and Spain. Historically, however, many nations have experienced fluctuations in replacement levels and still have managed to survive. Despite the drop in births, the United Nations predicts an increase in populations in Australia, Canada, China, France, Ireland, Norway, and the United States.

David Pearce Snyder, a renowned futurist and editor of *The Futurist Magazine*, sees a positive side to the movement.[28] He sees childlessness as merely an indication of our cultural modernization. He points out that our reasons for having children have changed over time. Whereas in earlier days children were needed to support a family, social safety nets (such as Medicare and Social Security) have taken care of those needs. Therefore, we now have children out of desire, not necessity. Conversely, he says that those who do not want children should not have them: "I think people who do not have children because they are wise enough to say they will not be good parents is an indication of the maturing of our society." He feels certain the entire society will benefit from this fundamental change. Snyder claims the family is the most adaptive institution in society. He goes on to say that this new development toward childlessness gives us the opportunity to expand the extended family. He points to the tremendous communications that families now have on the Internet via e-mail, for example, and sees that as a step in the right direction. For Snyder, the future is bright and the development of childlessness is an indication that our civilization is moving in the right direction.

I do not believe we are going to "slouch out of history" (Blankenhorn's term), but rather that we are engaging in more conscious reproduction. I see the move toward thoughtful parenting and conscientious childlessness as positive. For years, couples who enjoyed parenthood were on the defensive if they produced more than the approved 2.5 children. Conversely, women who were childless were derided for not producing. How much healthier to have a society with parents who want children having them and adults who do not, not doing so. And I do not agree that our society is fundamentally flawed. Rather, I believe it is evolving. I believe that as the childless revolutionaries develop their voice, some changes are inevitable. Politicians concerned with pleasing constituents will begin addressing some of the key issues that plague childless citizens, namely in the areas of taxes and housing. In the workplace, appropriate boundaries need to be established so that the working parent and the childless employee can each feel clear about what is expected of him or her. These retoolings will help create a more egalitarian society and one in which our citizenry will flourish.

The Population Reference Bureau reports, "The family has changed more in the last 10 years than any other social institution." It will continue to change. "Today's young women struggle with how they can achieve a balance in their lives . . . they will propel us forward, not backward."[29] Childlessness is part of that balancing act.

Society, it would seem, reinvents itself when necessary. "We are in a revolution," Snyder declared. " Historians will write about this decade in years to come. Remember, the world is orderly and makes sense. It is all about change."[30] We just have to recognize it—and embrace it.

Now We Know

Our reluctance to approve of childlessness stems from ignorance. If I don't know it, I don't like it. If I've never seen it before, I don't trust it. If it's not the way I do things, it can't be right. In the past, we have not had a clear picture of who was childless and why. We can no longer make that claim.

Doomsayers predicted terrible consequences when women entered the workforce, when divorce became more acceptable, when birth control became available. But for the most part, the consequences of liberation have been positive. More women than ever are choosing a life that does not conform to the old standard. The time has come to absorb into our consciousness a new version of femaleness, one that is predicated on the measure of a woman's character, not on the issue of her body.

PERSONALLY SPEAKING

Old-fashioned ways which no longer apply to changed conditions are a snare in which the feet of women have always been entangled.

—JANE ADDAMS[1]

5

Personally Speaking

As the mother of a fifteen-year-old girl, I wrestled with the notion that this work may make it easier for my child to choose childlessness—and I wondered if I wanted to do that. Certainly, part of me would like her to know the joy I have known mothering her. But then, parenting may not be her choice, and I would never want her, or her child, locked in that unhappy dance. Nor do I wish her to wind up tragically childless, having spent so much time building a career that she ignores a portion of her life she wrongly assumes she can attend to when she is ready.

I watch my stepdaughters, remarkable women in their thirties, grappling with their own reproductive choices. Both would like children; neither is married. Like the women who are childless by standards, they feel the need to provide a child with a father. But I have begun to hear new notes creeping into our conversations. They wonder how they will react when their own biological clocks begin to wind down. Do they forfeit the experience of having children? they wonder aloud. Do they dare shoulder the responsibilities alone? They are confused.

One of my stepdaughters has a friend whose marriage failed. Single again at thirty-nine, she knew time was running out. I was devastated for her when the marriage abruptly ended. She lost two dreams at once: a marriage and a family.

Years later, when she decided to have in vitro fertilization, a part of me understood her deep need to follow her heart's desire. But another part of me, a stronger, less articulate side, was concerned. I myself made the decision not to have a child when I was single. I could not do it because I was uncomfortable with a child not having a father—not even a deadbeat, sporadically visiting kind of dad; no physical person you can look in the eye and even tell off if you need to; no grave to visit; no photo album to pore over to see where the resemblance is. I think fathers matter in the lives of children. I see in my own child the benefits of her having the yin/yang, male/female to learn from and deal with. I think it makes her more prepared for life. But I look at my stepdaughters and worry the experience they so long for will pass them by. I know the amount of love they would lavish on a child. And suddenly I feel a chink in my armor. My need to see them happy begins to supersede my concerns about a child having a father. I am not yet ready to relinquish my values, but I sense the shift within me.

Mothering these days is a more complicated goal than it was even twenty years ago when I was contemplating it.

Many women have told me that the men they date are reluctant to commit to marriage and children. This puts these women—and my stepdaughters—in the difficult position of deciding whether they should parent alone. If they decide not to, their childlessness may well make them inadvertent casualties of modern trends in mating.

My exploration into the childless world has had an unexpected and very personal effect on my life. I feel a bit like a street sweeper, clearing the road for the marathon runners who are eager to begin the race. I finish my job and rush to the stands to watch as the women swiftly pass me by. There, in the midst of the crowd, I spot the familiar brown curls of my daughter. And I pray I have found every pebble in the road so that she does not trip. I did not anticipate when I began that exploring childlessness would possibly make life better for my daughter. But that, ultimately, is what I hope happens. I would like her decisions in life, whatever they may be, to be respected, and her choices considered as valid as anyone else's.

Notes

Author's Note

1. "Childless Couples," *American Demographics* (December 1993): 34.
2. Betty Friedan, *The Feminine Mystique* (New York: Norton, 1963): 20.

Introduction

1. Quoted in Elaine Partnow, *The Quotable Woman, 1800–1981* (New York: Facts on File, 1982): 298.

2. Quoted in Brenda Stalcup, *The Women's Rights Movement: Opposing Viewpoints* (San Diego, Calif.: Greenhaven Press, 1995): 149.

3. *Historical Statistics of the United States: Colonial Times to 1970* (Washington, D.C.: U.S. Bureau of the Census, 1973): 499.

4. David Dender and Bruno Leone, *Women's Rights Movement* (San Diego, Calif.: Greenhaven Press, 1995): 159.

5. Betty Friedan, *The Feminine Mystique* (New York: Norton, 1963): 87.

6. *Historical Statistics*, 385.

7. *Statistical Abstract of the United States: 1997* (Washington, D.C.: U.S. Bureau of the Census, 1998): 481.

8. Quoted in "I've Lived the Life I Wanted To," *Ladies Home Journal* (November 1992): 72.

9. Luchina Fisher, Steve Dale, and Sabrina McFarland, Untitled cover story, *People* (September 12, 1994): 86.

10. "Childless Couples," *American Demographics* (December 1993): 34.

11. *Statistical Abstract*, 87.

12. Gail Sheehy, *New Passages* (New York: Random House, 1995): 43.

13. *Statistical Abstract*, 202.

Chapter 1

1. Quoted in Women's History by Jone Johnson Lewis, About.com.

2. Ann Landers, *Wake Up and Smell the Coffee* (New York: Villard, 1996): 107–108.

3. J. Muncie, "Am I Missing Something Here?" Online posting: Child-free by Choice, America on Line (August 17, 1998).

4. Shere Hite, *The Hite Report on the Family* (New York: Grove Press, 1994): 174.

5. Leslie Lafayette, *Why Don't You Have Kids?* (New York: Kensington Books, 1995): 157.

6. "Trivia," *Childless by Choice Newsletter* (Vol. 4, No. 3, Summer 1996): 6.

7. Lafayette, *Why Don't You*, 158.

8. Ann Landers, "Ann Landers," *Los Angeles Times* (August 5, 1998): B12.

9. Elizabeth Badinter, *Mother Love: Myth and Reality* (New York: Macmillan Publishing, 1980): 316.

10. "Abnormal Maternal Behavior and Growth Retardation Associated with Loss of the Imprinted Gene *Mest*," *Nature Genetics* (October 1998): 167.

11. Bettijane Levine, "A Haven of Learning and Stability; School on Wheels Offers Homeless Children Help with Classwork and Supplies," *Los Angeles Times* (September 28, 1999): PE1.

12. Matthew Yee, "Charles Dederich, Founder of Cult-Like Religious Group Synanon, Dies at 83," Associated Press, http://www.aracnet.com/~atheism/rw/dederich.htm (March 5, 1997).

13. Marla Cone, "Growth Slows as Population Hits 6 Billion." *Los Angeles Times* (October 12, 1999): 6.

14. Zero Population Growth, "Complete Statement of Policy," www.zpg.org/whoweare.htm.

15. Ibid.

16. Stephanie Nebehay, "Yankee Rat Race," *ABC News*, http://abcnews.go.com/sections/us/Daily News/ilo_americans.html (February 1, 2000).

17. Patt Morrison, "Who Will Heed the Warnings on the Population Bomb?" *Los Angeles Times* (September 5, 1999): B3.

18. U.S. Bureau of the Census, "World Population Profile: 1998," www.census.gov:80/ipc/www/wp98001.html (January 29, 2000).

19. Christopher S. Wren, "United Nations: Population Slows," *New York Times* (October 21, 1998): A8.

20. Ben J. Wattenberg, "The Population Explosion Is Over," *New York Times Magazine* (November 23, 1996): 60.

21. Rosemarie Gillespie, "When No Means No: Disbelief, Disregard and Deviance as Discourses of Voluntary Childlessness," *Women's Studies International Forum* (Vol. 23, No. 2): 223–234.

22. Planned Parenthood Federation of America, Inc., "Emergency Hormonal Contraception Facts Sheet," www.plannedparenthood.org/library/BIRTHCONTROL/EmergContraHistory.htm (January 26, 2000).

23. Gina Kolata, "Without Fanfare, Morning-After Pill Gets a Closer Look," *New York Times* (October 8, 2000): 1, 18.

24. B. Pillsbury, F. Coeytaux, and A. Johnson, *From Secret to Shelf* (Santa Monica, Calif.: Pacific Institute for Women's Health, 1999): Preface.

Chapter 2

1. Anne Taylor Fleming, *Motherhood Deferred* (New York: G. P. Putnam, 1994): 254.

2. Diane Lore, "The Baby Chase," *Atlanta Constitution* (December 22, 1997): B1.

3. InterNational Council on Infertility, "National Summary and Fertility Clinic Report," www.inciid.org (1998): 1.

4. U.S. Centers for Disease Control and Prevention, "National Fertility/Infertility/Reproductive Health Summary," cdcinfo.cdc.gov (1995): 1.

5. Ibid.

6. U.S. Centers for Disease Control and Prevention, "National Center for Health Statistics," www.cdcinfo.gov (August 1993): 2.

7. Wayne Sinclair, "Infertility and Miscarriage Research Summaries," Environmental Causes of Infertility, www.chem-tox.com/infertility/: 1.

8. Madelyn Cain, *First Time Mothers, Last Chance Babies* (Far Hills, N.J.: New Horizon Press, 1994): 24, 25.

9. Gail Sheehy, *New Passages* (New York: Random House, 1995): 95.

10. American Society for Reproductive Medicine, "Guidelines for the Provision of Infertility Services," www.asrm.org/current/policy/provis.html (July 20, 1996): 1.

11. "Baby Boom, Baby Bust," *Pittsburgh Post Gazette*, www.post-gazette.com/babyboom/facts.asp (1995): C14.

12. Clomid is a fertility drug prescribed to induce ovulation; IVF means in vitro fertilization; GIFT means gamete intrafallopian transfer; ZIFT is zygote intrafallopian transfer (InterNational Council on Infertility, "National Summary").

13. Liz Tilberis, *No Time to Die* (New York: Little, Brown & Company, 1998): 116.

14. Tilberis, *No Time*, 116.

15. Fleming, *Motherhood Deferred*, 254.

Chapter 3

1. Quoted in Elaine Partnow, *The Quotable Woman, 1800–1981* (New York: Facts on File, 1982): 769.

2. Quoted in Henry Maier, *Three Theories of Child Development* (New York: Harper & Row, 1965): 38.

3. Bruno Bettelheim, *The Uses of Enchantment* (New York: Knopf, 1976): 201.

4. Tony Crespi and Ronald M. Sabatelli, *Children of Alcoholics and Adolescence* (New York: Libra Publishers, 1997): 408.

5. *Psychology Today* (March–April 1996): 20.

6. Arthur Jones, "Parting Is Sweet Sorrow for Activist Couple, Kids," *National Catholic Reporter* (September 26, 1977): 6.

7. John Bowlby, *The Making and Breaking of Affectional Bonds* (London: Tavistock, 1979): 133.

8. U.S. Bureau of the Census, "Percent Childless," www.census.gov/population/socdemo/fertility/fert95/tabH1.txt (November 25, 1997).

9. "Celebrities: Ingrid Bergman," *Mr. Showbiz*, http://mrshowbiz.go.com.

10. "Celebrities: Sophia Loren," *Mr. Showbiz*, http://mrshowbiz.go.com.

11. U.S. Centers for Disease Control and Prevention, "Data for 1996 Welfare Reform Law," www.cdc.gov/nchswww/whatsnew/bonus.htm (August 1999): 3.

12. Ann Hovarth and H. Elizabeth Peters, "Welfare Waivers and Non-Marital Childbearing," Joint Center for Poverty Research, www.jcpr.org/wp/Wpprofile.cfm?ID=131 (January 2000): 2.

13. Eric Nagourney, "Study Finds Families Bypassing Marriage," *New York Times* (February 15, 2000): B3.

14. Ariel Halpern, "Poverty Among Children Born Outside of Marriage," The Urban Institute, www.newfederalism.urban.org/html/discussion99-16.html (1999): 1.

15. American Psychological Association, "Family and Relationships: Single Parenting and Today's Family," http://helping.apa.org/family/-single.html (1996).

16. Elaine Campbell, *The Childless Marriage: An Exploratory Study of Couples Who Do Not Want Children* (London and New York: Tavistock, 1985): 143.

17. *Statistical Abstract of the United States: 1975* (Washington, D.C.: U.S. Bureau of the Census, 1975): 42; *Statistical Abstract of the United States: 1997* (Washington, D.C.: U.S. Bureau of the Census, 1997): 65.

18. J. Bernard, *The Future of Marriage* (New York: Bantam, 1972): 60–63.

19. J. Veevers, *Childless by Choice* (Toronto: University of Western Toronto, 1980): 29.

20. Campbell, *The Childless Marriage*, 140.

21. Interview with Dr. Margaret Rubin, Beverly Hills, Calif., September 29, 1999.

22. "10 Ways to Tell Your In-Laws," *Childless by Choice Newsletter* (Vol. 2, No. 1, 1994): 1.

23. *Barbie Bazaar Magazine* (February 1998): 114.

24. Linda Wason-Ellam, *If Only I Was Like Barbie* (Paper presented at the National Council of Teachers of English Conference on College Composition and Communication, Urbana, Ill., October 1997): 430.

25. Ibid.

26. Joyce C. Abma and Linda S. Peterson, *Voluntary Childlessness Among U.S. Women: Recent Trends and Determinants* (Paper presented at the Annual Meeting of the Population Association of America, April 6–8, 1995).

27. "Childless by Choice: Can I Live a Rich, Balanced Life Without Joining the Parenthood Procession?" *Health Magazine* (March–April 1996): 98.

28. Elaine Tyler May, *Barren in the Promised Land* (New York: Basic Books, 1995): 11.

29. Mardy Ireland, *Reconceiving Women: Separating Motherhood from Female Identity* (New York: Guilford Press, 1993): 7.

30. Jan Cameron, "Without Issue," University of Canterbury, New Zealand, www.regy.canterbury.ac.nz/publish/research/97/A18.htm (1999).

31. Ireland, *Reconceiving Women*, 1.

Chapter 4

1. Quoted in Elaine Partnow, *The Quotable Woman, 1800–1981* (New York: Facts on File, 1982): 66.

2. Alfred, Lord Tennyson, quoted in Angela Partington, ed., *The Oxford Dictionary of Quotations* (New York: Oxford University Press, 1996): 683.

3. U.S. Bureau of the Census, Fertility and Family Branch, "Childless Women, Ages 15–44,"personal communication, 1999.

4. Paula K. Clarke, *Intended Childlessness, Silent Protest, and Revitalization Potential* (Monograph presented at the 97th annual meeting of the American Anthropological Association, Philadelphia, December 2–6, 1998): 4.

5. Tanya Koropeckyj-Cox, "Loneliness and Depression in Middle and Old Age: Are the Childless More Vulnerable?" *Journals of Gerontology, Series B: Psychological Sciences and Social Sciences* (Vol. 53B, No. 6, November 1998): 303–312.

6. The chance of a woman achieving a pregnancy when she is between fifteen and twenty-four years of age is 92 percent. From age twenty-five to thirty-four, it drops to 65 percent, and between thirty-five and forty-four it is 34 percent (J. C. Abma, A. Chandra, W. D. Mosher, L. Peterson, L. Piccinino, "Fertility, Family Planning, and Women's Health: New Data from the 1995 Survey of Family Growth," National Center for Health Statistics, *Vital Health Statistics* [Vol. 23, No. 19, 1997]). Even if an older woman does achieve a pregnancy, the miscarriage rate for a fifteen- to twenty-four-year-old is 4 percent, whereas a forty-five-year-old has a 50 percent risk (Wayne Sinclair, "Infertility and Miscarriage Research Summaries," Environmental Causes of Infertility, www.chem-tox.com/infertility/).

7. "A Big Boost in Multiple Births," *Los Angeles Times* (September 27, 1999): C1.

8. Rick Weiss, "Menopausal Woman Gets Ovary Implants," *Los Angeles Times* (September 24, 1999): 22.

9. Quoted in Gorton Carruth and Eugene Ehrlich, *The Harper Book of American Quotations* (New York: Harper & Row, 1988): 251.

10. Elinor Burkett, *The Baby Boon: How Family-Friendly America Is Cheating the Childless* (New York: The Free Press, 2000): 147.

11. Ibid., 150.

12. Quoted in Marnell Jameson, "Do Childless Workers Get the Short End of the Stick?" *Los Angeles Times* (March 13, 2000): E1, 3.

13. Carol M. Anderson and Susan Stewart, *Flying Solo: Single Women in Midlife* (New York: W. W. Norton, 1994): 156.

14. Ibid., 157.

15. Interview with Alyce Bonura, IRS enrolled agent, Ojai, Calif., September 30, 2000.

16. U.S. Department of Housing and Urban Development, "Fair Housing . . . It's Your Right," www.hud.gov/fhe/fheact.html: 1–6.

17. Quoted in Joanna Powell, "Oprah's Awakening," *Good Housekeeping* (December 1998): 114–115.

18. Associated Press, "Ms. in Marital Bliss," www.abcnews.go.com (September 6, 2000).

19. Ruth Ashby and Deborah Gore Ohrn, *Herstory* (New York: Viking, 1995): 112.

20. Ibid., 132.

21. Interview with Noel Riley Fitch, Los Angeles, Calif., April 20, 2000.

22. Jennifer Uglow, *The Continuum Dictionary of Women's Biography* (New York: Continuum, 1989): 290.

23. James King, *Virginia Woolf* (New York: W. W. Norton, 1994): 407.

24. Ashby and Ohrn, *Herstory*, 122.

25. Stephen B. Oates, *A Woman of Valor: Clara Barton and the Civil War* (New York: The Free Press, 1994): 25.

26. Jane Addams, *Jane Addams: A Centennial Reader* (New York: Macmillan, 1960): ix, x, xi.

27. Interview with David Blankenhorn, Institute for American Values, New York, September 22, 2000. Interview with Tom Smith, director of Social Survey at the University of Chicago, Chicago, September 25, 2000.

28. Interview with David Pierce Snyder, *The Futurist Magazine*, Bethesda, Md., September 23, 2000.

29. Population Reference Bureau, *Population Bulletin* (Vol. 51., No. 3) www.prb.org/pubs/population_bulletin/bu51-3/ahead.htm (December 1996).

30. Interview with Tom Snyder.

Chapter 5

1. Quoted in Elaine Partnow, *The Quotable Woman, 1800–1981* (New York: Facts on File, 1982).

Bibliography

Books

Aburdene, Patricia, and John Naisbitt. *Megatrends for Women*. New York: Villard Books, 1992.

Addams, Jane. *Jane Addams: A Centennial Reader*. New York: Macmillan, 1960.

Anderson, Carol M., and Susan Stewart. *Flying Solo: Single Women in Midlife*. New York: W. W. Norton, 1994.

Anderson, Paul. *Janet Reno: Doing the Right Thing*. New York: John Wiley & Sons, 1994.

Apter, Terri. *Secret Paths: Women in the New Midlife*. New York: W. W. Norton, 1995.

Ashby, Ruth, and Deborah Gore Ohrn. *Herstory*. New York: Viking, 1995.

Badinter, Elizabeth. *Mother Love: Myth and Reality*. New York: Macmillan, 1980.

Barone, Michael, and Grant Ujifusa. *The Almanac of American Politics 1998*. Washington, D.C.: National Journal, 1997.

Bender, David, and Bruno Leone. *Feminism—Opposing Viewpoints*. San Diego, Calif.: Greenhaven Press, 1995.

Bernard, J. *The Future of Marriage*. New York: Bantam, 1972.

Bettelheim, Bruno. *The Uses of Enchantment*. New York: Knopf, 1976.

Bowlby, John. *The Making and Breaking of Affectional Bonds*. London: Tavistock, 1979.

Brady, Joan. *I Don't Need a Baby to Be Who I Am*. New York: Pocket Books, 1998.

Burkett, Elinor. *The Baby Boon: How Family-Friendly America Is Cheating the Childless*. New York: Free Press, 2000.

Cain, Madelyn. *First Time Mothers, Last Chance Babies*. Far Hills, N.J.: New Horizon Press, 1994.

Campbell, Elaine. *The Childless Marriage: An Exploratory Study of Couples Who Do Not Want Children*. London: Tavistock, 1985.

Carruth, Gorton, and Eugene Ehrlich. *The Harper Book of American Quotations*. New York: Harper & Row, 1988.

Crespi, Tony, and Ronald Sabatelli. *Children of Alcoholics and Adolescence*. New York: Libra Publishers, 1997.

Dender, David, and Bruno Leone. *Women's Rights Movement*. San Diego, Calif.: Greenhaven Press, 1995.

Engel, Beverly. *The Parenthood Decision*. New York: Doubleday, 1998.

Fabe, Marilyn, and Norma Winkler. *Up Against the Clock*. New York: Random House, 1979.

Faludi, Susan. *Stiffed: The Betrayal of the American Male*. New York: William Morrow, 1999.

Faux, Marion. *Childless by Choice: Choosing Childlessness in the Eighties*. Garden City, N.J.: Anchor Press, 1984.

Fleming, Anne Taylor. *Motherhood Deferred: A Woman's Journey*. New York: Putnam, 1994.

Friedan, Betty. *The Feminine Mystique*. New York: Norton,1963.

Genevie, Louis, and Eva Margolies. *The Motherhood Report*. New York: Macmillan, 1987.

Gilligan, Carol. *In a Different Voice*. Cambridge, Mass.: Harvard University Press, 1982.

Goldberg, Nancy, and Jill Tartule. *Women's Ways of Knowing*. New York: Basic Books, 1973.

Greer, Germaine. *The Female Eunuch*. New York: McGraw-Hill, 1971.

Historical Statistics of the United States: Colonial Times to 1970. Washington, D.C.: U.S. Bureau of the Census, 1973.

Hite, Shere. *The Hite Report on the Family*. New York: Grove Press, 1994.

Illich, Ivan. *Gender*. New York: Pantheon, 1982.

Ireland, Mardy. *Reconceiving Women: Separating Motherhood from Female Identity*. New York: Guilford Press, 1993.

Kasper, Shirl. *Annie Oakley*. Norman and London: University of Oklahoma Press, 1992.

King, James. *Virginia Woolf*. New York: W. W. Norton, 1994.

Kline, S. *Out of the Garden*. Toronto, Ontario: Garamound Press, 1993.

Lafayette, Leslie. *Why Don't You Have Kids?: Living a Full Life Without Parenthood*. New York: Kensington Publishing, 1995.

Landers, Ann. *Wake Up and Smell the Coffee*. New York: Villard, 1996.

Lisle, Laurie. *Without Child: Challenge the Stigma of Childlessness*. New York: Ballantine, 1996.

Maier, Henry. *Three Theories of Child Development*. New York: Harper & Row, 1965.

Marsh, Margaret. *The Empty Cradle: Infertility in America from Colonial Times to Present*. Baltimore: Johns Hopkins University Press, 1996.

May, Elaine Tyler. *Barren in the Promised Land: Childless Americans and the Pursuit of Happiness*. New York: Basic Books, 1995.

Morell, Carolyn. *Unwomanly Conduct*. New York: Routledge, 1994.

Noble, June, and William Noble. *How to Live with Other People's Children*. New York: Hawthorn Books, 1977.

Oates, Stephan B. *A Woman of Valor: Clara Barton and the Civil War*. New York: The Free Press. 1994.

Partington, Angela, ed. *The Oxford Dictionary of Quotations*. New York: Oxford University Press, 1996.

Partnow, Elaine. *The Quotable Woman, 1800–1981*. New York: Facts on File, 1982.

Peck, Ellen, and Judith Senderowitz. *Pronatalism: The Myth of Mom & Apple Pie*. New York: Crowell Company, 1974.

Pillsbury, B., F. Coeytaux, and A. Johnson. *From Secret to Shelf*. Santa Monica, Calif.: Pacific Institute for Women's Health, 1999.

Popcorn, Faith, and Lys Marigold. *Clicking*. New York: HarperCollins, 1996.

Richardson, Mark, ed. *Frost—Collected Poems, Prose & Plays*. New York: Penguin, 1995.

Safer, Jeanne. *Beyond Motherhood: Choosing a Life Without Children*. New York: Pocket Books, 1996.

Sheehy, Gail. *New Passages*. New York: Random House, 1995.

Stalcup, Brenda. *The Women's Rights Movement: Opposing Viewpoints*. San Diego, Calif.: Greenhaven Press, 1995

Statistical Abstract of the United States. Washington, D.C.: U.S. Bureau of the Census, various years.

Stern, Daniel. *The Interpersonal World of the Infant*. New York: Basic Books, 1985.

Stern, Sydney Ladensohn. *Gloria Steinem: Her Passions, Politics, and Mystique*. New York: Carol Publishing, 1997.

Tilberis, Liz, with Aimee Lee Ball. *No Time to Die*. New York: Little, Brown, 1998.

Uglow, Jennifer. *The Continuum Dictionary of Women's Biography*. New York: Continuum, 1989.

Veevers, J. *Childless by Choice*. Toronto: University of Western Toronto, 1980.

Wolf, Naomi. *Fire with Fire: The New Female Power and How It Will Change the 21st Century*. New York: Random House, 1993.

Periodicals and Reports

Abma, J. C., A. Chandra, W. D. Mosher, L. Peterson, L. Piccinino. "Fertility, Family Planning, and Women's Health: New Data from the 1995 Survey of Family Growth." National Center for Health Statistics, *Vital Health Statistics*. 1997. Vol. 23, No. 19.

Abma, Joyce C., and Linda S. Peterson. *Voluntary Childlessness Among U.S. Women: Recent Trends and Determinants*. Paper presented at the Annual Meeting of the Population Association of America, April 6–8, 1995.

"Abnormal Maternal Behavior and Growth Retardation Associated with Loss of the Imprinted Gene *Mest*." *Nature Genetics*. October 1998: 167.

Avins, Mimi. "Showing That Compassion Is Always in Fashion." *Los Angeles Times*. May 7, 1998: E1.

Barbie Bazaar Magazine. February 1998: 114.

Benedetti, Faith. "A Reflection on the Untried Womb." *Sage Woman*. December 31, 1996: 22.

"A Big Boost in Multiple Births." *Los Angeles Times*. September 27, 1999: C1.

"Childfree Housing Planned." *Childless by Choice Newsletter*. Summer 1996. Vol. 4, No. 3: 1.

"Childless by Choice: Can I Live a Rich, Balanced Life Without the Parenthood Procession?" *Health Magazine*. March–April 1996: 98.

"Childless Couples." *American Demographics*. December 1993: 34.

"Childless Women, Ages 15–44." Fertility and Family Branch, U.S. Bureau of the Census, personal communication, 1999.

Clarke, Paula K. *Intended Childlessness, Silent Protest, and Revitalization Potential*. Monograph presented at the 97th annual meeting of the American Anthropological Association, Philadelphia, December 2–6, 1998.

Cone, Marla. "Growth Slows as Population Hits 6 Billion." *Los Angeles Times*. October 12, 1999: 6.

Day, Terry. "Childfree Media Notes." *Childless by Choice Newsletter*. Summer 1996. Vol. 4, No. 3: 3.

Fisher, Luchina, Steve Dale, and Sabrina McFarland. Untitled cover story. *People*. September 12, 1994: 86.

Gillespie, Rosemary. "When No Means No: Disbelief, Disregard and Deviance as Discourse of Voluntary Childlessness." *Women's Studies International Forum*. Spring 2000. Vol. 23, No. 2: 223–234.

Grace, Catherine O'Neill. "How & Why: Understanding a Parent's Illness." *Washington Post*. August 3, 1999: Z17.

"I've Lived the Life I Wanted To." *Ladies Home Journal*. November 1992: 72.

Jameson, Marnell. "Do Childless Workers Get the Short End of the Stick?" *Los Angeles Times*. March 13, 2000: E1, E3.

Jones, Arthur. "Parting Is Sweet Sorrow for Activist Couple, Kids." *National Catholic Reporter*. September 26, 1977: 6.

Kolata, Gina. "Without Fanfare, Morning-After Pill Gets a Closer Look." *New York Times*. October 8, 2000: 1, 18.

Koropeckyj-Cox, Tanya. "Loneliness and Depression in Middle and Old Age: Are the Childless More Vulnerable?" *Journals of Gerontology, Series B: Psychological Sciences and Social Sciences*. November 1998. Vol. 53B, No. 6: 303–312.

Landers, Ann. "Ann Landers." *Los Angeles Times*, August 5, 1998: B12.

Levine, Bettijane. "A Haven of Learning and Stability; School on Wheels Offers Homeless Children Help with Classwork and Supplies." *Los Angeles Times*. September 28, 1999: PE1.

Lore, Diane. "The Baby Chase." *Atlanta Constitution*. December 22, 1997: B1.

Massad, Stewart, M.D. "Brave, Braver, Bravest." *Discover*. November 1999: 43.

McMenamin, Brigid. "The P.C. Enforcers." *Forbes*. February 10, 1997: 86.

Morrison, Patt. "Who Will Heed the Warnings on the Population Bomb?" *Los Angeles Times*. September 5, 1999: B3.

Nagourney, Eric. "Study Finds Families Bypassing Marriage." *New York Times*. February 15, 2000: F8.

Nason, Ellen, and Poloma, Margaret. "Voluntary Childless Couples." *Sage Research Papers in the Social Sciences*. 1976. Vol. 5: 47.

Pogash, Carol. "The War Between Women: Working Mom's Juggling Act Has Earned Her Some Surprise Enemies." *Chicago Tribune.* October 8, 1989: 1.

Powell, Joanna. "Oprah's Awakening." *Good Housekeeping.* December 1998: 114–115.

"Scotching Marriage." *Psychology Today.* March–April 1996: 20.

Smith, Tom W. *American Sexual Behavior.* Chicago: National Opinion Research Center, December 1994.

"10 Ways to Tell Your In-Laws." *Childless by Choice Newsletter.* 1994. Vol. 2, No. 1.

"Trivia." *Childless by Choice Newsletter.* Summer 1996. Vol. 4. No. 3: 6.

"Unfair Taxes and the Workplace." *Childless by Choice Newslette.*, N.d.

U.S. Bureau of the Census, Fertility and Family Branch. "Childless Women, Ages 15–44." Personal communication, 1999.

Wason-Ellam, Linda. *If Only I Was Like Barbie.* Paper presented at the National Council of Teachers of English Conference on College Composition and Communication, Urbana, Ill., October 1997: 430–436.

Wattenberg, Ben J. "The Population Explosion Is Over." *New York Times Magazine.* November 23, 1996: 60.

Weiss, Rick. "Menopausal Woman Gets Ovary Transplant." *Los Angeles Times.* September 24, 1999: 22.

Wren, Christopher S. "United Nations: Population Slows." *New York Times.* October 21, 1998: A8.

Zamichow, Nora. "A Parent's Dread: Learning She Was Pregnant Set Off Months of Anguish for a Woman with AIDS and Her Husband." *Los Angeles Times.* October 17, 1998: 1.

Electronic Resources

American Psychological Association. "Family and Relationships: Single Parenting and Today's Family." http://helping.apa.org/family/single.html. 1996.

American Society for Reproductive Medicine. "Guidelines for the Provision of Infertility Services." www.asrm.org/current/policy/provis.html. July 20, 1996.

Associated Press. "Ms. in Marital Bliss." www.abcnews.go.com. September 6, 2000.

"Baby Boom, Baby Bust." *Pittsburgh Post Gazette*. www.post-ga-zette.com/babyboom/facts.asp. 1995.

Cameron, Jan. "Without Issue." University of Canterbury, New Zealand. www.regy.canterbury.ac.nz/publish/research/97/A18.htm. 1999.

"Celebrities: Ingrid Bergman." *Mr. Showbiz*. http://mrshowbiz.go.com.

"Celebrities: Sophia Loren." *Mr. Showbiz*. http://mrshowbiz.go.com.

Futurework. "Trends and Challenges for Work in the 21st Century." www.dol.gov/dol/asp/public/futurework/report/chapter3/main2.html.

Halpern, Ariel. "Poverty Among Children Born Outside of Marriage." The Urban Institute. www.newfederalism.urban.org/html/discussion99-16.html. 1999.

Haney, Daniel Q. "Drugs Reduce AIDS Risk." *ABC News*. abcnews.go.com.

Hovarth, Ann, and H. Elizabeth Peters. "Welfare Waivers and Non-Marital Childbearing." Joint Center for Poverty Research. www.jcpr.org/wp/Wpprofile.cfm?ID=131. January 2000.

InterNational Council on Infertility. "National Summary and Fertility Clinic Report." www.inciid.org. 1998.

"Mary Pickford: The Jewel in the Crown." www.mdle.com/Classic Films/FeaturedStar.

Muncie, J. "Am I Missing Something Here?" Posted on Childfree by Choice, America on Line. August 17, 1998.

Murray, Kathleen. "The Childless Feel Left Out When Parents Get a Lift." *New York Times Service*. www.childfree.net/leftout.html. 1996.

National Centers for Health Services. FEDSTATS. www.cdc.gove/nch-sww/datawh/statab/pubd/2319_49.htm.

Nebehay, Stephanie. "Yankee Rat Race." *ABC News*. http://abcnews.go.com/sections/us/DailyNews/ilo_americans.html. February 1, 2000.

Planned Parenthood Federation of America, Inc. "Emergency Hormonal Contraception Facts Sheet." www.plannedparenthood.org/library/BIRTHCONTROL/EmergContraHistory.htm. January 26, 2000.

Population Reference Bureau. *Population Bulletin*. Vol. 51, No. 3. www.prb.org/pubs/population_bulletin/bu51-3/ahead.htm. December 1996.

Presbyterian Outreach. Presbytel.ctr.pcusa.org. February 18, 2000.

Schramm, Richard. All American Baptist Church. Richard.Schramm@abc-usa.org. February 18, 2000.

Sinclair, Wayne. "Infertility and Miscarriage Research Summaries." Environmental Causes of Infertility. www.chem-tox.com/infertility/.

United Nations Population Fund. "The State of the World Population 1999." http://www.unfpa.org/about/unfpa.htm. January 27, 2000.

U.S. Bureau of the Census. "Percent Childless." www.census.gov/population/socdemo/fertility/fert95/tabH1.txt. November 25, 1997.

_____. "World Population Profile: 1998." www.census.gov:80/ipc/www/wp98001.html. January 29, 2000.

U.S. Centers for Disease Control and Prevention. "Data for 1996 Welfare Reform Law." www.cdc.gov/nchswww/whatsnew/bonus.htm. August 1999.

_____. "National Center for Health Statistics." www.cdcinfo.gov. August 1993.

_____. "National Fertility/Infertility/Reproductive Health Summary." cdcinfo.cdc.gov. 1995.

U.S. Department of Housing and Urban Development. "Fair Housing . . . It's Your Right." www.hud.gov/fhe/fheact.html.

Women's History by Jone Johnson Lewis. About.com.

Yee, Matthew. "Charles Dederich, Founder of Cult-Like Religious Group Synanon, Dies at 83." Associated Press. www.aracnet.com/~atheism/rw/dederich.htm. March 5, 1997.

Zero Population Growth. "Complete Statement of Policy." www.zpg.org/whoweare.htm.

_____. "Who We Are and What We Are About." www.zpg.org/whoweare.htm. November 1, 1998.